Thomas Poplaws
practising psychol
has taught and pei
and has published articles in numerous magazines
and journals on topics in education, psychology and
the arts.

To my teachers in Ringwood and Botton Village
and to the members of both of those
Camphill communities who so
generously support the arts.

Thomas Poplawski

Eurythmy

Rhythm, Dance and Soul

Floris Books

First published in English in 1998 by Floris Books

© 1998 Thomas Poplawski
Thomas Poplawski has asserted his right under the
Copyright, Designs and Patents Act 1988
to be identified as the Author of this Work.

Front cover photograph by Werner Schliske
Back cover photograph by Aliki Sapountzi

British Library CIP Data available

ISBN 0–86315–269–4

Printed in Great Britain
by Cromwell Press, Trowbridge, Wilts.

Contents

Acknowledgments

My warmest appreciation is to my eurythmist wife Valerie for her advice and editorial assistance throughout the entire project. The book is very much hers as well as my own.

In exploring the history of modern dance I am much indebted to the book of Joseph H. Mazo, *Prime Movers*. For the section on eurythmy therapy I have Seth Morrison and Rachael Ross to thank for helpful conversations that we had.

Finally, let me thank Ronald Kotzsch for his continuing support and encouragement in learning the ways of the publishing world.

Thomas Poplawski

1. From Temple Dance to Modern Art

Dance is an independent rhythm, a movement whose centre is outside of the human being. The rhythm of dance takes us to a primeval age of the world. The dances of our time are a degeneration of the original temple dances that embodied knowledge of the most profound secrets of the world.[1]

With these words Rudolf Steiner expressed the essence of the renewal he was to bring to the art of dance with the founding of the movement art of eurythmy. Still little known in the English-speaking countries, this art of 'en-souled movement' has grown since its founding earlier in the century to include some thousands of eurythmists around the world. Eurythmy is found gracing the stages of grand theatres, most impressively by the large stage groups in Amsterdam, Hamburg, Stuttgart, and Dornach (Switzerland), but also in another form in schools, clinics, and in communities for those with special needs. For what this art has achieved is a kind of 'unified field theory' of artistic movement, providing a nucleus which inspires and en-kindles a performing art, an educational approach for children and adults and, finally, a movement therapy used as an adjunct to medical and psychological treatment.

Remarkably, Rudolf Steiner (1861–1925), was not him-self a dancer but rather an inspired philosopher, writer, playwright, scientist, and veritable Renaissance man who founded the movement called Anthroposophy or spiritual science in Germany in 1913. Steiner believed that with the ending of what in Sanskrit was called the *Kali Yuga* or

*Helena
Petrova
Blavatsky
(1831–91)*

Dark Age in the late nineteenth century, the time had come to reopen the ancient Mysteries to humanity, to reveal what had for millennia remained the secret property of occult societies. This revelation of the Mysteries had already begun with the discovery and translation of sacred texts from the East and their subsequent popularization, and with the spiritually channelled revelations of Helena Petrovna Blavatsky, founder of the Theosophical Society. This trend has continued throughout the century up to the present time when a person can walk into any bookstore and find shelves of books expounding occult teachings and practices. Steiner's interest, however, was not merely in discovering the nature of the old Mysteries or attempting to reconstruct them. Rather, he strove to reinfuse spirituality and deeper meaning into a western culture that had turned too onesidedly toward a materialistic worldview by reviving the Mysteries in a manner that would be appropriate for the individual of today. He set about doing so through inspiring contributions, often of revolutionary calibre, in philosophy, the arts, and the sciences. The renewal of the art of dance was one to which he attributed especial importance not only for the arts but in the rejuvenation of the spiritual-cultural life in general. In order to understand what Steiner was attempting in his creation of eurythmy, it would be important to take an historical survey of dance especially in regard to its origin in the Mysteries, and to the thread which was apparently lost, but which Steiner hoped to pick up in his reinvention of the art.

Dance and the Mysteries

Dance is regarded as the oldest of the arts, requiring only the body as its instrument. Like all of the arts, it was considered to be a gift to the human race from the spiritual worlds, from the realm of the hierarchies of angels or the gods. In the Greek tradition, Terpsichore, who inspired dance, was one of the nine Muses, all daughters of Zeus, leader of the Titans, and Mnemosyne, the goddess of Memory. Though all the Muses shared in song and dance, it was Terpsichore who brought this gift to Earth.

Just as the child learns to gesture and to walk before speaking, so is it believed that communication began in earliest times through movement. Sympathy with another was expressed through imitating and mirroring the movement of the other, bringing the two into an understanding harmony and concordance. Then one or the other would lead the 'conversation' in a particular direction with the other following initiating a dance which went back and forth between the two. Inspiring this interchange was the presence and movement of the natural world and the cosmos above, as well as the inhabitants of these realms. Communication in ancient times was not so obsessed with the mere practicalities of asking someone to 'pass the butter!' In the few writings which have come down to us from earliest times the impression of the early human being is not one of a lumbering, unshaven Neanderthal, but rather of a not entirely physical creature reminiscent of some Tolkienian forest folk, living in harmony and with resonance and extreme sensitivity to others and the natural world around.

Steiner (in his book *Cosmic Memory*) described all human beings of these times as clairvoyant, meaning that their thinking and deeds were influenced and inspired by spiritual forces and beings on a quite conscious level, though this consciousness was rather dreamlike and ethereal by modern standards. The earth was kept in harmony through the guidance given humanity by these gods, through the communities mirroring in movement impulses received from on high, then creatively elaborating this impulse through the dances they performed with each other. This life in Paradise, however, eventually came to an end. The Biblical story of Adam and Eve relates the expulsion from the Eden of this shared life with the spiritual realm. After this time, the human connection to the spiritual worlds began to dim. This loss of spiritual guidance could be seen as a necessary step in human development. If every action of an individual were ordained by spiritual beings, the 'pressure' of divine presence would never have allowed the development of free will and the freedom of choice which we value so highly.

This loss, however, left the ancients in fear and confusion. Without a direct experience of the will of the gods, how were they to decide on rules of social conduct or morality, how were they to know when to plant, to harvest, to remain in synchrony with the divinely inspired rhythms of nature, of Gaia?

Certain individuals still maintained an openness to the inspiration of the spiritual world. The Old Testament is filled with stories of sages and prophets visited by angels or even, as with Moses on Mount Sinai, by a higher level of spiritual being, Yahweh or Jehovah. Many of these individuals had undergone training in special schools called

Dancing maenads (Second century BC)

Mystery centres, the mysteries implied being those of maintaining a connection between everyday consciousness and the more spiritual one. In these centres, specialized instruction was given and successful candidates were administered rites of initiation which reopened spiritual sight and hearing. In this fashion, for some time the link with the old gods was preserved. In time, however, even the Mysteries began to decay. As the consciousness of humanity dimmed, it became the role of the Mysteries and a clairvoyant priesthood to direct what now became rituals. As such, this was also the time when the arts (and artists) came into being. Prior to this time when everyone enjoyed the clairvoyant capacity to receive impressions from spiritual realms, the communicating and inspiring function of the arts was unnecessary. With the coming of the Dark Age, however, the arts sprung forth from the Mystery temples as a means of continuing to transmit the sacred will, especially through rites and rituals. In ancient Greece this took the form of the dithyramb or circular chorus *(chorus being Greek* for 'dance') celebrated in the *orchestra* (Greek for 'dancing place'). Originally, the entire village gathered around a central altar, singing and dancing in

Ballet

rhythm, moving in one direction for the verse and in the opposite direction for the repeated refrain. In time, as the Mysteries became decadent and lost their efficacy around the ninth to tenth centuries BC, these rituals were often limited to a group of the men, while the rest of the village watched, creating for the first time an audience. In Athens the dithyramb was celebrated by fifty men or boys with a standardized form to the ceremony. After the ritual failed on a number of occasions to bring abundant crops, it began to lose its magical appeal. However, this creation of the audience, the switching from the orchestra to the theatre (from *theatron* or 'seeing place'), led to the form that drama and the performing arts utilize even today.

As the spiritual senses faded, human beings were pushed into a kind of aloneness, isolated within themselves and into acting more as individuals rather than through being commonly inspired as a group. Dance followed this pattern, for the first time taking on the role of a profession and, in western culture, predominantly one of men. Just as verbal teachings were preserved in the Mystery temples along with techniques for accessing the words of the gods, so too were the dances the preserve of the temple. As such, the formerly spontaneous activity that was imminently inspired now became frozen into precisely memorized movements for which the temple dancer was trained. A training in technique and aesthetic sensitivity developed which restricted experimentation or an individual's personal inspiration by the Muse. The importance of adhering to the prescribed form is underlined in one example: in the New Hebrides, any dancer making a mistake was assaulted, wounded, or even killed by bowmen posted to watch for any inaccuracy in the rituals. Another example, in this case from music, comes from the ancient Chinese text, *Shu King.* There is described how the Emperor Shin traveled throughout the country testing the exact pitch of the music played in the various districts, checking that the music was in perfect correspondence with the five tones of their pentatonic scale. It was taught that if the districts began to tune their instruments differently, the peoples themselves would begin to differ and to fight among themselves. Such strictures placed on the performance of the arts thus arose from the fear that any deviations from the formula once revealed by those who could experience the spirit would cause the gods to withdraw their blessing and beneficence from that tribe or people. Interestingly, remnants of these old Mystery dances can still be found, from Hopi reservations to temples in Bali to the movements which the Caucasian Greek sage, G.I. Gurdjieff, brought back from his 'Meetings with Remarkable Men' in Central Asia.

Secular dance

To judge from numerous pictures and hieroglyphics, there was no evidence of social dancing in ancient Egypt and this was apparently so elsewhere. Dance was solely a sacred activity as were the other arts. The secular aspects of the arts would only come about once the Mysteries had decayed. At the outset, even social dancing strove for the ideals of engendering communal harmony and enacting the 'dance of the planets' here on earth as evidenced in the circle dances of the Middle East and the Morris dancing of the English Cotswolds. Dance eventually became entirely secular in the West, falling even to the level of sexual hedonism in ancient Rome, a true desecration of an art form once given by the gods for an entirely different purpose. Except for the scattered remnants of the old temple dances and their vestiges preserved in some folk dances, no perpetuated stream carried the dance from its early origins (much less further developed this original impulse). Dance was enjoyed for the delight which bodily movement can bring in social and folk dancing and continued in this form for centuries until its revival as a controlled dramatic art in the late sixteenth century with the birth of ballet.

Ballet was a child of an era in which the intellect sought to civilize the wildness of nature, whether that be in the French garden which assumed meticulous orderliness and an

Sergei Diaghilev (left) with Igor Stravinsky during their Ballet Russe collaboration

elaborate geometric plan, or that of bodily movement, which ballet provided with a set of rules and forms with the aim of giving grace to the body. This included the training of unnatural positions which were espoused as beautiful — the 'turn out' of the knees to show the leg in profile even when the dancer faced forward or the dancing on the toes in specially designed slippers. This was the first time in which the dance was again appreciated as a serious art form in the West. The development of its series of canonical positions and poses with the dancer moving in prescribed ways from one position to the next gave it a classical underpinning, but by the end of the nineteenth century it had become rather academic.

Russian ballet stars Anna Pavlova and Mikhail Mordkin

Tradition that later degenerated into empty convention weighed down ballet and brought a number of dancers to view it no longer as a viable art form. Ballet had instead become a matter of grandiose and empty showmanship — accentuating technical brilliance and acrobatics. Somehow the inner core of the art of dancing had been lost sight of, replaced by an outer show of the number of pirouettes a ballerina could perform and how long she could remain poised on her toes, or how high a male dancer could leap. Ballet received a new lease on life in the twentieth century with the forming of Sergei Diaghilev's *Ballets Russes*. Choreographers like Michel Fokine, and dancers like Nijinsky and Anna Pavlova took the impulse from dance revolutionaries like Isadora Duncan and brought about a revitalization of ballet. However, they were unable to overcome some of the basic flaws of the art form, a classical rigidity which condemned it to remain a child of the intellectual age which gave it its birth.

Against this backdrop, a new storm in dance was

brewing, led primarily by a group of American women dancers, though it was in Europe that they brought their revolution.

Dance in the twentieth century

Growing up in America, a number of talented young women felt drawn by this Muse of dance but, of the theatrical dancing that they had the opportunity to experience, the ballet seemed academic and rigid in its adherence to its five positions while show-dancing seemed frivolous, even empty-headed. These were women who sought to dance in a manner which was based on natural forms of body movement and which allowed them to express the deeper impulses of the human soul.

Isadora Duncan (1878–1927) was probably the most famous and flamboyant of these disciples of a new art. She sought to free dance from the structures of following the music, of being entrapped in form. She saw the mission of dance as expressing pure emotion by the body, the mad innocence of Dionysian ecstasy. She turned to the Greeks as her model for a new dance, studying statues, friezes, and vases in an attempt to revive that spirit which once propelled the dance. She danced barefoot and in Greek dress and was a woman of tremendous vitality. She condemned ballet for teaching form without content but in her own attempt to form a school of dance, beginning with her young stage group 'the Isadorables,' she met failure — hers was condemned as a dance of content without a teachable form. Nevertheless, the legacy which she bestowed was to freely dance music and not just dance to music, pointing to the inner wisdom which lies within the music itself.

Loie Fuller (1864–1928) was another of the young women who destabilized the set notions of dance. Discarding the traditional tights, she wrapped herself in long, flowing garments dyed in myriad colours and became a creator of imaginative forms. She later extended her experimentation to include changing coloured lights, an innovation only now possible with the advent of a new technology of electric lighting. In her 'Fire Dance' she performed standing on a sheet of glass, lit from below as she gyrated and moved flowing silks above, evoking a living flame for her audience below. Though she was credited with being quite mediocre as a dancer, she stretched the definition of dance beyond the physical body of the individual dancer to encompass the animating and organizing of space, a space enlivened by colour in movement.

Ruth St Denis (1877–1968) was a third force in the birth of twentieth century 'modern dance.' Her earliest exposure to dance was in lessons in the teachings of François Delsarte (whom Duncan had also studied), a philosophy and method of pantomime which became a fad in America in the late nineteenth century. The method brought the honest expression of emotion to movement. Its popularity, unfortunately, degenerated into stock poses of emotional states, like 'Despair' and 'Defiance.'

She went on to study dance with various teachers afterwards and was influenced by both Duncan and Fuller. Her strongest inspiration, however, came from her fascination with the ancient cultures of the East. She commented when she saw the dancing of a Japanese performer:

> Her dancing was the antithesis of the flamboyant,
> overblown exuberance of our American acrobatics.
> Here was a costuming in which the colours were
> vivid, yet so related to the mood that they
> seemed to emanate from a different palette.
> Her performance haunted me for years.[2]

This feeling impelled St Denis to study the little then available on the ancient Mystery cultures of the East and the surviving remnants of their temple dances. The fruit of these studies she brought to the stage in a series of images of ancient cultures, of Egypt, India and, later, of Japan. In contrast to the sparse costuming of Duncan, St Denis evoked a sumptuous spectacle bedazzling to the senses. Hers was a dance embedded in crowd-pleasing stagecraft, where

Isadora Duncan (1878–1927)

lighting, incense, elaborate costumes and stage sets helped to evoke a mood. Her first impulse was a search for the primal source of the dance but she also insisted on making hers a popular art — the sight of her bared midriff in those Victorian times was said to have brought in as many viewers as the dancing. As with Isadora Duncan, sexuality and sensuality were inextricably linked with the dance in the imagination of the public.

Another innovation she introduced was that of 'music visualization' in her Synchoric Orchestra. Unlike her other 'story dances,' this was a plotless dance in which every performer corresponded to an instrument and moved when it played. Her imagination for this form of dance stemmed from her memories of Duncan's dancing of the Unfinished

Ruth St Denis and her dancing partner Ted Shawn

Symphony. Doris Humphrey and later dancers took up the concept of music visualization in group choreography although it changed from her conception. St Denis was a dancer whose ideal was mystical and, in a somewhat romanticized manner, understood dance as a religious experience though she also felt the need to cater to the popular taste. She helped to elevate dance from mere acrobatic tricks, bringing it close to religion and true art through using what has always captured the audience even in Shakespeare — sexuality and 'show business.'

With the contributions of these three pioneers, the face of dance was transformed. They brought a new idea to what the art could be, releasing it from old conventions and forms and in the process somehow rediscovering some of the soul of dance. Theirs was a lyrical exploration in search of beauty and inspired by the roots of the art in ancient times as they imagined it. They brought little to the art in the way of technique but nevertheless were able to rekindle an appreciation for dance as an art form. With the opening that they created, marvellous new opportunities presented themselves which several dance 'streams' attempted to take advantage of. As has already been mentioned, ballet received a new lease on life through its incorporation of some of their ideas, though it has still remained somewhat of a charming antiquity. The primary heiress, however, has been that amorphous field called 'modern dance' and, more recently, 'contemporary dance.' The impulse of these early pioneers was taken up but transformed, as we shall see, in a fashion that has probably fallen short of their original intent.

Modern and contemporary dance

With the advent of the First World War, the western world became a changed place. The old order politically, socially, and culturally came to an end and, in a way, a certain innocence and idealism were lost. Part of this change manifested in the taking up of a different picture of the human being, that of Sigmund Freud, which was to have a profound effect on our view of human motivation. Along with a popularization of the ideas of Charles Darwin and the later theories of behaviorism, a range of philosophies had a significant impact on the emerging new forms of dance.

Mary Wigman (1886–1973) had studied in Switzerland with two great theorists, Jacques Dalcroze and Rudolf von Laban. Dalcroze had founded a system for helping dancers and music students to develop a sense of rhythm by translating sound into physical movement. His system, called Eurythmics (often confused in name with eurythmy), never fully evolved into a dance form but is still quite popular with student musicians.

In 1914, Wigman came to study with Rudolf von Laban and became his assistant. Von Laban had through his studies of movement devised a manner of coding and notating dances just as music is written. Breaking every movement down into component parts can create a vocabulary of movement which could become rather analytically stilted. In her own evolving use of Laban notation, Wigman sought to emphasize the ability of the body to become capable of performing any movement demanded of it. She trained her dancers athletically, employing gymnastic exercises. In contrast to the musical lyricism of Duncan or St Denis, she trained her dancers to work without music or to the accompaniment of percussion. She found great inspiration in the Expressionist movement which was sweeping the German art circles of the time, emphasizing a breaking away from tradition (including the tradition that held that art should be beautiful) to present deeply experienced 'subjective truths.'

Martha Graham (1895–1992) further transformed the direction of dance by shifting its profile from that of a concert to that of a dramatic performance, moving it away from the lyricism of pure dance movement to the more intellectual, introspective, dramatic realm. She was much influenced by psychoanalytic theory and sought through dance to delve into the mysterious realm of subconscious

Martha Graham, pioneer of modern dance

impulses and *Id,* seeking to plumb the depths of mind and body. Like the earlier dancers, she had an interest in religious themes but this was coloured by Freud's views of human motivation. She sought to find freedom for the dancer through the expression of emotion, and by exploring a body freed of societal strictures. Music was no longer so much to dance 'to' as the dancer trying to 'get inside' the music and subjectively to express it. In his book, *Modern Times,* Paul Johnson credits Graham with setting 'an individualist American ideal,' emphasizing the personalization of the dance to express every dancer's self.

There have been other geniuses in the formation of modern dance in the second half of the century but with the two figures we have mentioned a picture arises from which one might already characterize what came later. We need in this regard to speak of some main themes and influences that are evident, for unlike ballet which presents one system modified by different teachers, modern dance embraces many systems.

First, there has been an increase in the physicality of dance since early in the century, such that dance has come to be associated with athletic rigour. For the pioneers of this century, this would be viewed as a throwback to the acrobatic dancing which they strove to eclipse, missing the point that they sought to somehow transcend the physical body.

There has been a 'psychologizing' of dance mirroring the influence of Freud on the intellectual community, which is disturbing because of the way these theories reduce the image of the human being to that of a mere puppet of the instincts. On one level this has taken the form of psychological theories being enacted. On another level there has been the acceptance by many of the theory that one's subjective emotional states must be 'worked through' via the body, that it is important to express one's subjective experience. This is a rather old problem in the arts — even in the instructions which Leonardo gave to young painters in his notebooks, he addresses the need to become more and more of an artist. He points out that the inexperienced painter always reproduces himself in his paintings while the more experienced painter is able to bring the being of the world into art. With the psychoanalytic worldview as an artist's foundation, it can be difficult to find this 'being of the world,' instead the artist may become locked in an unending internal struggle or Sisyphean dilemma with no apparent escape — the purpose of dance becomes a public psychotherapy session.

Finally, in contemporary dance, there has been a frantic search for inspiration to every conceivable source, from remnants of the old Mystery dances to folk dances of every culture, to martial arts, even to the mechanistic movements of the robot. This can sometimes be amusing but suggests an unsettling lack of a centre to which all the pieces are related. Even ballet has been returned to by many contem-

Contemporary dance

porary dancers, perhaps because of the 'stability' which its tradition provides or to the anchor of its strict vocabulary and logically derived structure.

In a way this tendency returns dance to the questions posed by the early innovators: is there a higher set of laws which govern the dance (beyond the intellectual constructs of ballet), laws which indicate the meaning, purpose, and direction of dance? It also begs the question as to whether, despite the popularity of dance, the art form has lost its way, is merely thrashing about in search of a core, has either sunken into a morass of subjective experimentation, physical acrobatics, or mere entertainment — the dangers

that Duncan, Fuller, and St Denis sought to transcend. One
fears that somehow the impulse of these great pioneers has
been sidetracked; that despite the genius of its leaders and
the spiritual aspirations of many of its practitioners modern
dance has not formed of itself a vessel that could carry
these aspirations; that contemporary dance has somehow
failed in its most profound mission.

2. Another Direction

Late in 1912, Rudolf Steiner was approached by a woman named Clara Smits who had been following his lectures for a number of years with interest and now sought his counsel. Her husband had unexpectedly died only two weeks before, and she was concerned about finding a career for her eighteen-year-old daughter, Lori. One of her daughter's interests was dance and gymnastics. Steiner suggested that something could be done along those lines on an anthroposophical basis and that he would be willing to instruct her.

This instruction formed the beginnings of the new art of eurythmy (from the Greek for 'beautiful' or 'harmonious movement'), another stream of dance which sought to reconnect with the original impulse of Terpsichore; to continue the revolution begun by the pioneers of the twentieth century dance (without necessarily being their direct descendant); to restore dance to its original role as a mouthpiece for the spiritual, revealing the workings of higher laws while manifesting those laws on earth through the art form. With the end of the Dark Age in the late 1800s, Steiner foresaw a resurgence in spirituality in the West as many individuals would begin to have clairvoyant experiences, visions of angels and other non-material beings, visions of the afterlife, and so on. Humanity would require help and guidance in crossing over this mysterious threshold to spiritual consciousness, as the almost universal acceptance of the materialistic worldview meant that those having spiritual experiences were left confused, upset, and fearful that they were going mad. Steiner feared that dance would follow the materialistic streams of the twentieth century which concern themselves with only a limited

Lori Maier-Smits

aspect of reality and human experience. He felt that a new art of movement was needed that would take advantage of this historic opportunity by reintroducing the light of the ancient Mysteries. The role of this new art was to guide humanity in crossing this threshold through developing an expanded view of reality, going beyond the purely materialistic.

Questions then arise as to what is this expanded conception, what are these objective spiritual laws, this non-materialistic *Weltanschauung* that was to inspire the new art of eurythmy?

The hidden laws of movement

Rudolf Steiner felt strongly that only through art was a general renewal of social and cultural life possible. Even before the upheaval caused by the First World War, Steiner sensed a deterioration of the cultural life, an alienation from the truth which the arts had once helped to instill as a guiding influence toward human values and ideals.

In his own time he saw the attempts which artists made toward breaking away from stale conventions but falling short of attaining a reconnection with the stream of spirituality. In Impressionism, the painter sought to reproduce the immediate impression, according to Steiner, because the modern individual had lost the ability to penetrate to the inner nature of things as great artists of earlier epochs could still do. Impressionism speaks to the senses and to visual perception but somehow limits itself to conveying only a surface prettiness. Expressionism, on the other hand, depicted all that arose chaotically from the inner life, often with little regard for what was aesthetically pleasing. It strove to reveal the subjectively experienced inner at all costs culminating in the exposition of raw emotion in the later Abstract Expressionism. Steiner felt that true art needed to find a middle ground between these two extremes of Impressionism and Expressionism, jubilating in the

aesthetics of the natural realm while simultaneously revealing the wisdom that lay beneath.

Steiner had an extensive background in the arts. He had
edited a literary journal in Berlin for a number of years for
which he also acted as an art critic. As Berlin was a major
cultural centre of Europe at that time, he was well placed to
appreciate the latest artistic currents and experiments. He
directed a number of plays including some by his friend, the
French writer Edouard Schuré, as well as those of his own
creation, his series of four Mystery Plays. He pursued an
interest in painting while his lectures on colour were quite
influential to an important group of other painters including
Vasily Kandinsky and Franz Marc. He also worked with
artists and craftspeople to create new approaches in such
varied disciplines as sculpture, poetry, architecture, singing,
instrument making, and jewelry design, always with the
intent of bringing renewal to the arts.

Steiner was especially inspired by the writer, poet, and
dramatist, Johann W. von Goethe. Celebrated as the 'Shakespeare of the German language,' Goethe was less well
known for his numerous scientific studies including *The
Metamorphosis of Plants* and his anti-Newtonian theories of
light and colour. Steiner had been trained as a scientist and
philosopher and taken an early interest in this aspect of
Goethe's work which led to his being asked to edit the
scientific writings for the prestigious Weimar edition of
Goethe's complete works.

In the founding of a new movement art, Steiner referred
to his inspirer:

> Eurythmy takes its start from Goethe's view that all
> art is the revelation of concealed laws of Nature,
> which, without such revelation, would remain
> concealed. This thought may be connected with
> another Goethean thought. In each human organ
> there is an expression of the 'whole' form of man.
> Each human limb is, as it were, the human being in

Rudolf Steiner in 1916 >

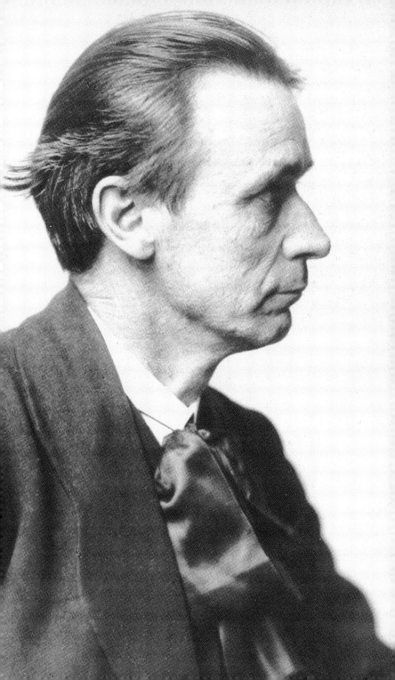

Edouard Schuré

miniature. We may reverse this though and see in man a complete expression of what one of his organs represents. In the larynx and the other organs connected with speech and song, these activities set up the movements or the tendency to movements which are revealed in sounds or combinations of sounds, although the movements themselves are not perceived in ordinary life. It is not so much these movements themselves but the 'tendencies' to them which are to be transformed by eurythmy into movements of the whole body. What occurs imperceptibly in the formations of sounds and tones in a single system of organs is to become visible as movement and posture in the whole human being.[3]

In trying to understand how eurythmy seeks to surmount this polarity of Impressionism-Expressionism through finding some higher level synthesis, it seems that the key lies in these 'movement tendencies' behind speech and its formation by the larynx. Let us examine what is meant by these mysterious 'tendencies,' referred to by Steiner as the forces of the 'etheric.'

The etheric realm

When we speak, or when a violin string is plucked, the air moves in a fashion invisible to the eye. The ear, however, can hear these movements and interpret them. Rudolf Steiner was able to perceive forms that accompanied or vibrated with the movements in the air. These he attributed to the etheric or life realm which surrounds and enlivens the earth and all living things.

The etheric realm has long been known and, in ancient times, even directly perceived by gifted individuals,

A scene from one of Steiner's Mystery Plays

An early eurythmy group: Emica Senft (Mohr), Friedel Simons (Thomas) Maria Schuster (Jenny)

especially by those who work with living things like the farmer or the healer. In our own age of materialism, this rarified nonphysical realm has for the most part been shrugged off as superstition or as the unknowable 'laws of nature' until quite recently. Asian medicine, by contrast, has long acknowledged the existence of *chi* or *ki* as a central aspect of the healing arts as well as recognizing its importance in movement in Asian martial arts. In the 'internal disciplines' of *Kung-Fu (Tai-chi Chuan, Pakua,* and *Hsing-i),* for instance, as in eurythmy, these tendencies or etheric forces are consciously transformed into movement. In the language of the martial arts, first one senses the *chi* and allows it to precede, and then the physical body fills the space it has imaginatively created.

Modern science has begun to approach this ancient teaching through theories like the 'Gaia hypothesis' of James Lovelock and Lynn Margulis which addresses the etheric sheath surrounding and nourishing the being of the earth, and in experiments like those with the Kirlian auras which can be detected by instruments examining living things.

When we look at a human being, what presents itself to our physical senses is the 'physical body' of the individual. This body we can touch and see, even taste, just as we can a stone. The 'etheric body' underlies the physical. In the case of the stone, there is no etheric body which enlivens it and grants it a sentient quality as there is in the case of the plant. As such, the plant is already subject to the mysterious laws of the living realm, and not merely those of matter. A corpse portrays the physical body bereft of the etheric; it soon decays as it is now subject only to the laws of matter and no longer regenerated by the life forces. For that is the very nature of the etheric realm — life-giving, life-creating forces.

The ancients imaginatively pictured this wellspring of all life as a burgeoning, spiralling, ever moving energy that never rests. They attempted to portray this experience of the etheric in such forms as the carvings in the initiation chambers which archaeologists call 'chambered tombs' at

Newgrange in Ireland or the Isle of Gavrinis in Brittany
(apparently misnamed as both of these show no evidence of
ever having been used for burial). Though they fixed these
images in stone, they knew that the etheric never rests, but
pulses continuously in ordered and harmonious movement.

Another image for the etheric is found in the term 'the
water of life' for it is to the liquid element that it bears
most affinity. In the swirl or meander of the running stream
one senses the signature of the life realm. In the spiral of a
whirlpool of wind or water (sometimes frozen into fixed
image in the calcified form of a sea creature like the
Nautilus or the shell of the watery snail) one perceives just
one of the archetypal patterns of the ether. This pattern has
been repeatedly used through the ages on pottery and
adorning jewelry and clothing as an icon of the primal life
force. In the steady roll of the waves on the sea one
experiences the rhythmical flowing of the etheric which the
artist has rendered through the beat and rhythm of music or
even the harmonious knotwork patterns in Celtic art.

Still another aspect of both water and the ether is its
ever-changing, ever-transforming nature, a seemingly ran-
dom quality of metamorphosis which nevertheless appears
to follow certain laws. Only recently studied by science
under the name of 'chaos theory,' this aspect of the ether
was portrayed by the ancient Greeks in the figure of the
sea-god Proteus, who magically assumed one form after
another, like the sea, never fixed, ever changing. Steiner felt
that a true art form, in the tradition of the Mysteries, is one
which manifests the workings of spirit through matter,
revealing the underpinnings of natural laws. As Steiner
explains:

> ... when one is watching eurythmy, one ought to be
> able to sniff nature in all of it, and surmise the
> spirit in all of nature ... One can imagine that
> someone seeing eurythmy could say: That eurythmy
> movement reminds me of an impression I had the
> other day when I was walking through the woods,
> of a fir tree swaying in the wind. If he does not

The spiral stone at the entrance of Newgrange, Ireland

simply keep to this feeling but later is able to say:
Yes, eurythmy has finally given me an explanation
of that fir tree; it is not standing there just to be a
fir tree, it is one letter in the eternal Word that
surges and weaves through the world, eurythmy
explains to me how the fir tree speaks, how the
brook speaks, how the lightning speaks ...[4]

Steiner's intent was that eurythmy would encompass
these qualities of the etheric, its abundance of enlivening
forces, its pulsing rhythmicity, its swirling and spiralling, its
metamorphosis of Protean forms. In consciously manifesting
these forces, it could thus be an art of movement that was
life enhancing, life-rejuvenating, even healing. But at the
same time it was to be an art form that had to do with 'the
eternal Word that surges and weaves through the world.'
This special relationship with how nature 'speaks' and the
connection of the etheric to speech in general is one which

Marie Steiner

we must examine next if we are to understand just how eurythmy goes about accomplishing its mission as a vehicle of the numinous 'Word.'

The Word

> In the beginning was the Word, and the Word
> was with God, and the Word was God. The same
> was in the beginning with God. All things were
> made by him: and without him was made nothing
> that was made. In him was life, and the life was
> the light of men.[5]

From the beginning, eurythmy was developed not out of music but out of the 'Word.' The role of movement in eurythmy was to make speech 'visible' and to express and amplify the hidden laws behind it. This brings us to the special relationship that exists with the larynx (to which we alluded in the earlier quote from Goethe) and, in turn, to try to understand the nature of this sacred 'Word.'

The larynx as the organ of speech has always held a special position in mystical lore. In ancient India it was considered the center of higher creativity through the wheel of power or *chakra* that is etherically associated with it. The ninety year old leader of the ashram at Auroville in India, a Frenchwoman affectionately called 'the Mother,' announced in the 1970s that she would actually give birth via the larynx, though she died without this occurring. The principle behind her statement is that just as the physical larynx creates the uniquely human phenomenon of speech, so is the etheric larynx a centre for creative life-force activity.

Language and speech were at one time more alive and more imbued with spiritual potency than is the case today. Like the arts, they were originally deemed to be gifts of the gods because they represented a reflection of divine activity here on earth. The Word or Logos is the term which refers to the primal creative force of the spirit. Speech, as an earthly child of the Word, originally had no outer 'practical'

*Rudolf Steiner's sketches of two eurythmy figures
depicting the sounds 'B' (left) and 'S'*

function but was rather a manner in which human beings
participated in the creative activity of the gods. The ancient
reverence for the power of speech stemmed from the
original potency of words as magical vessels of formative
life energies. The 'naming of things' was an especially
important activity as was the knowing of their secret true
names because of the power this bestowed on its possessor,
be it the 'true name' of God (amongst the ancient Hebrews)
or, in fairy tales, the true name of Rumpelstilskin! Similarly
the speaking of spells and incantations were once able to
evoke actual changes in weather or the health of a living
being through their influencing of the life forces.

   With the passage of the ages, speech became more a
servant of communicating earthly concerns and less a vessel
of the forces of life, or an extension of the activity of
spiritual forces. In eurythmy and in a revived art of recitation and speech which he founded with his wife, Marie,
Rudolf Steiner sought to resurrect the livingness which
speech once embodied. He felt that an enlivened speech

could tap the energetic force of the Word as portrayed in the prologue to St John's Gospel. Through its activity of making speech visible, eurythmy could enhance the viewer's experiencing of the primal creative forces of the Word, in the process revealing both the hidden laws of speech as well as those of nature. In this manner, dance could reassume its role in the Mysteries of leading humankind toward a more balanced view of reality, one encompassing both spirit and matter.

In actuality, all forms of movement, be they dance, gymnastics or athletics, work on some level with the etheric forces. What distinguishes eurythmic movement is that, on one hand, as in the early dance pioneers of the century, these forces were not so 'tied up' with the musculature which keeps them rather earth bound. Instead, like speech and music, they move with the air, seeking a home somehow between heaven and earth. Steiner once explained that:

> ... [through the eurythmical gestures'] overcoming of gravity in the human movement organism, one lifts their existence out of the earthly and expresses their soul being in such a way that there is affirmed in every single gesture: I am carrying in my earthly being a heavenly being! [And later goes on to conclude that] eurythmy unchains the eternal human being out of the earthly one.[6]

Another difference in the way that eurythmy accesses and uses these life forces is that it does so more consciously as a result of the guidance Steiner was able to bestow through his own ability to discern these forces as well as training others to attain such sensitivity. For both of these reasons, the eurythmist has a greater possibility of making use of these energies to create an art form both enlivening and healing. This healing aspect was later to be put into practice in educational and therapeutic applications of the art that are refined to a degree that modern and contemporary dance have not come close to achieving.

Visible speech

The movements of eurythmy unfold as the body acts as an
expanded larynx, shaping the air as the larynx does invisibly
when we speak. This shaping of the air and of space
follows the laws of natural creation, the laws of the Word.
In making speech visible, eurythmy 'outpictures' for the
viewer not only the outer content of the speech but all that
underlies it, i.e. the otherwise hidden laws of the realm of
life and Nature. The building blocks of speech, to begin
with, are the sounds of the letters of the alphabet. Each
sound when spoken has the effect of shaping the air (and
with it the ether) in a unique and specific manner. According to the ancient Mysteries, each of these sounds represented one aspect of the working of the formative power of
the life force, and as the archaic human being spoke or
heard one of these sounds one resonated with and re-

A eurythmy exercise with copper rods

experienced the force. The magic of the alphabet was such that it described not in an abstract manner but dynamically the total human experience of the natural world around.

In consonantal sounds one experiences most strongly the outer aspects of natural experience from the most dramatic elemental forces of storm and sea to the delicate movements of the swaying seaweed. In a sound like 'sh' we can still hear the rushing and frothing of waters, while the 'r' carries a general sense of movement, especially in the continental, trilled version of the sound. The active and formative nature of the consonants can most be experienced in onomatopoeic words like 'splash' or in the old Germanic or Saxon alliterative verse as found in works like *Beowulf*. In the vowel sounds we find more an expression of the inward emotional experience of the individual. The sound of 'ah' metaphorically expresses the same openness in feeling as the physical opening of the mouth which we perform in making the sound. Because they can act as such vehicles of our inner experience, we often utter vowel sounds even without words to express ourselves whether in sighing, laughing or expressing surprise, 'Oh!'

In everyday speech the original intent of speech has often been lost or forgotten. This living expression of inner and outer nature is still captured in the works of some poets and playwrights and the attentive listener still can partake of the rejuvenating and transformative etheric energies thereby. This process is enhanced and accentuated when speech is outpictured in eurythmic gesture through the moving of the sounds of a word or sentence; the etheric energies are once more experienceable and in the process speech is somewhat redeemed, regaining an iota of its former glory as vehicle of the Word. In practice, the beginning student of eurythmy initially moves the consonant sounds rather clumsily as if in semaphore (which is an example of speech made visible merely for the purpose of physical communication), stuck in a physical body framework of trying to make fixed forms of the sounds as if they were ballet positions. In time the student becomes more adept, more sensitive, and feels for herself the truth in the

gestures. They begin to move, to flow, to take on the process quality of the etheric realm rather than the stasis of the
physical. This becomes possible through the student's
entering of the imaginative, picturing realm of the etheric,
whereby one is lifted out of the more concrete consciousness of everyday existence into the fluid and vital world of
spiritualized or inspired thinking. In this sense, the study of
eurythmy is a training not only of the body but of the
consciousness of the student, enabling access to the realm
of 'feeling thinking,' an imaginative cognition which reveals
truths which one's normal cognition is too stiff or hardened
to access. In this respect, too, we see an echo of the mission
of the ancient Temple dance where, in the initiation of its
dancers, an elevation of the sensitivity and consciousness
allowed them to serve as a bridge to the gods.

The alphabet, as well as the words and sentences which
it forms, are not the only aspect of speech which are
worked with. Eurythmy goes deeper into language by working as well with its entire grammatical structure. Whereas
the gestures for the sounds of eurythmy are usually portrayed by the arms and sometimes the legs, other aspects of
grammar are revealed in the eurythmy 'form,' the pattern
that is moved through space. Grammatical forms like rhyme
schemes, the active or passive nature of a verb, accusative
or ablative cases, parts of speech, or the rhythm of a poem,
can all be artistically rendered though, like the grammar
itself, they tend to serve rather invisibly as the hidden
skeleton beneath, and not be the glaringly most evident part
of an artistic performance.

Within the development of what is distinguished as
'speech eurythmy,' Steiner sought a way of revealing
through art natural as well as supernatural or supersensible
truths. In addition to directing attention to the forces within
the earth, he also indicated the corresponding forces working from out of the cosmos for all true dancing, according
to Steiner, had its origin in the movement of heavenly
bodies which the dancer brought down to earth. He did this
through the indications which he gave for gestures for the
signs of the zodiac and for the seven original planets of the

ancients as well as movement forms including the 'Dance of the Planets.' He also gave correspondences between the consonants and the zodiac and the vowels and the planets. These lent another deeper, even esoteric aspect to the art but a true intuition of the 'music of the spheres' was only possible when eurythmy made another step, that of 'singing to music in movement.'

Visible music

In early demonstrations of eurythmy, this new art was met with some interest and enthusiasm but the constant question put to Rudolf Steiner was how eurythmy could also work with music. Steiner then set about establishing the foundations of 'tone eurythmy' which would seek to make visible in space what was normally invisible and only audible.

The grammar and alphabet of music are different from that of speech. Tone eurythmy had instead to work with the elements of pitch, rhythm, and beat as elements of its grammar with the actual musical tones and the intervals between the tones as its A to Z. In utilizing the human body as an instrument for 'playing' the music in space, Steiner chose to use the length (from head to toe) to express the pitch, the possibility of moving forward and backward and the polarity of the right and left sides of the body for the rhythm and beat, while the arms sang the tones and intervals. On an outer level, this could be mechanically performed by some marionette (and so it sometimes appears with a beginning student) but as the eurythmist learns to fill these movements with the being of her soul, we experience the music actually 'playing' and expressing itself through the eurythmist. What a contrast from the direction taken by modern and contemporary dance where the music is often seemingly either ignored or left behind in a dancer's subjective elaboration. Eurythmy was to strive to overcome the purely subjective, to sacrifice the eurythmist's egoistic experience in order objectively to portray the universal wisdom and power inherent in music and speech.

As in speech eurythmy, the sentences and paragraphs of music find their expression in the eurythmy form. For tone eurythmy, Steiner drew over a hundred 'standard forms' which have since served as basic models for students. They represent a kind of mapping of the music's meandering; like the wind moving through a forest they often possess an airy quality, a living stream of movement in space. The tone form expresses the skeletal grammar of the musical piece like the progression of musical motifs, the major and the minor modes, or the beat. These grammatical aspects may also reveal themselves in the way one eurythmist passes the theme to another — one example would be three groups moving together, representing the tonic, dominant, and sub-dominant chords with each taking its turn to carry the theme through moving more pronouncedly as that theme arose in the piece. Steiner used group movement in various ways including his own version of St Denis' Synchoric Orchestra. Each eurythmist moves the part of an individual instrument be it a duet or entire orchestra, enacting both the character and the tones of that instrument — as the flute has a very different sound from a trumpet, the quality of the movement would need to reflect this.

Eurythmy is always performed to live music (or speech) for the qualities which only live performances have — the spontaneous differences from one performance to the next, the energetic 'presence' of the musician, and the superior sound which recordings cannot manage to capture. Steiner was also asked about whether eurythmy could be put to song but he felt that this would pose a difficult situation. One could illustrate the musical part of the song but this would not address the words, a prospect Steiner considered inartistic. He felt that the eurythmy was itself a singing and had no need to be redundantly 'doubled.'

This synopsis of some of the basic principles of eurythmy may seem a bit abstract or difficult to comprehend. Hopefully, the examples given in the coming chapters describing the art's applications on stage, in education, and as a therapy will serve to make them easier to grasp.

3. On Stage

In performing eurythmy, the whole body must have become soul.[7]

Eurythmy had its first steps not in a dance studio or through public classes but rather with Rudolf Steiner's first indications given to Clara Smits for her daughter when Clara had come to speak to him at the end of 1911. As a beginning, he gave a single exercise for Lori:

> Tell your daughter to step alliterations. Let her make a forceful, somewhat stamping step to the alliterating consonant and a 'pleasing' arm movement whenever this consonant is absent. She should keep in mind that alliteration, properly speaking, occurred only in the North, that is, in countries where it is very windy. Let her imagine that an ancient bard is striding along the seashore, lyre in arm, amid the blast. Each step is a deed — a battle and a victory over the storm. And then he sets his fingers to the strings and joins his song to that of the wind.[8]

A few months later Steiner met briefly with Lori and added some preparatory studies for the work she was to enter — a study of human anatomy, of Greek art from the archaic to the classical periods with particular attention to be paid to the gestures and positions of the figures, and of what she could learn about Greek dance. He also directed her attention to a progression of figures found in an alchemical text of Agrippa von Nettesheim. She was told to learn

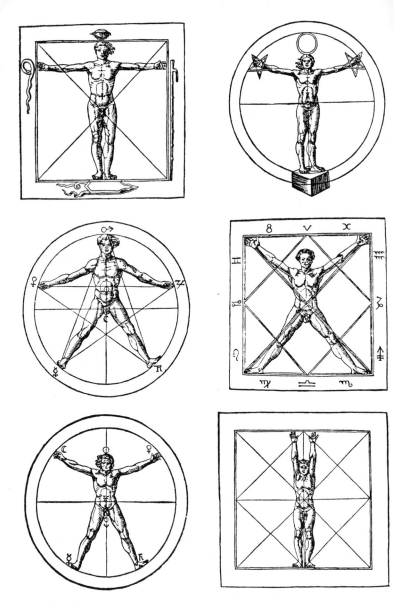

Figures from the alchemical text, De Occulta Philosophia, *by Agrippa von Nettesheim*

The eurythmy gestures of 'I' (ee) and 'O'

the progression and practice springing in succession from one position to the next (Steiner later added a phrase to accompany each position in this meditation in movement, beginning 'I think speech'). Finally, he gave her the exercise of writing with her foot (!) for the enlivening and bringing of more consciousness to the feet and not just the head.

Steiner was an extremely busy man and consistently overcommitted and was only able to finally follow up these preliminary instructions with his first formal lessons to Lori in the autumn of 1912. They met in Munich where he was working on presenting one of his Mystery Dramas at a Munich Theater Festival. There he gave her his first indications for working with the vowels I (ee), A (ah), and O. In her vivid recollection of the moment, Lori described how he allowed her to discover the sound gestures in her own form and how she was enabled to sense the etheric, formative forces. Her description was that of eavesdropping on the human body, 'listening' to the sounds of speech that are inscribed into the the body's laws of structure. As this occurs the sound-gestures are released from the human physical make-up and set free as soul-spiritual formative energies (i.e. one begins to move in resonance with the etheric forces or *chi* and not merely out of physicality). At their next meeting a few weeks later, Steiner expanded on this lesson on the vowels to include arm movements in expressing the vowel sounds, and in the coming months gave instructions for the forming of the other vowel and consonant sounds. At this next meeting he was accompanied by a colleague, Marie von Sievers (in future years she became his wife). Von Sievers was a Russian-born actress who worked intensively for years in the Anthroposophical Society with Steiner. Because of her background in the performing arts, she was much intrigued by the new impulse which Steiner was attempting to bring to dance. She was already involved in Steiner's work in drama and in reviving the art of speech and recitation. She was later to become a head teacher and director in a school of 'speech formation' and drama and eventually also to head the first training for eurythmists. Soon others stepped forward with interest in learning the new art and Steiner was able to begin small group forms on a circle. At that stage he gave the first short verse form for speech eurythmy, to a verse he had written called 'The Cloud Illuminator.' However, it was to be a while before eurythmy would mature enough to stand independently as a stage art. In the meanwhile, Steiner made use of this art of movement for the solving of certain difficulties he was having in producing scenes in his Mystery Dramas and the great *Faust* of Goethe. The problem in both of these was that utilizing costumed actors was unsatisfactory for the roles of spiritual beings or, in the case of *Faust,* Part II, entire scenes that take place beyond the earthly plane. Goethe's play was for this reason considered for many years to be unperformable. The later success with the piece was to make Dornach the Bayreuth for the performance of Goethe's work, due in part to the use of eurythmy to bring the hitherto impossible scenes to life.

The Goetheanum in Dornach

At the same time that eurythmy was coming into being, Rudolf Steiner was involved in another major undertaking, the designing and building of a home for the anthroposophical work, especially for the stagework of drama and eurythmy. After plans for a building in Munich were scrapped due to their rejection by city planning authorities, a rural property was offered on a hill near Basel in Switzerland. There, in Dornach in 1914, the erection of a building began which was to be named the *Goetheanum* after Steiner's main inspirer — an immense wooden structure topped by two interlocking domes covered in Norwegian slate. After the shell was completed, the long and laborious process of decorating the interior began at a time (with the coming of the First World War and the subsequent financial crises in Central Europe) when both workers and funds were in short supply. A series of tall columns of different types of wood surrounded the stage and auditorium spaces individually carved to Steiner's instructions, while above the curved ceilings were covered by expansive colour-saturated murals. Steiner referred to the building as the 'House of the Word' and spoke of a special connection to eurythmy — its stages were especially designed with its needs in mind but on a deeper level he expressed that he had 'feelingly created' the forms of the building from the same inward inspiration from which eurythmy arose.

Through the years of the First World War, hundreds of volunteers came to work on the structure and the interior slowly took shape. In order to accommodate the ongoing work in the performing arts while the interior work was going on, the large workmen's shed next to the Goetheanum was fitted with a stage and lighting. After the first Goetheanum was destroyed by arson in 1923, this simple shed was to host the developing eurythmy work for some time. In 1925, the striking *Eurythmeum* which Steiner had designed to provide studio space and offices was completed and continues to serve in this capacity today.

The first Goetheanum; to the right is the workmen's shed which was used as a stage

In 1914, a school of eurythmy was opened in Dornach and soon Marie von Sievers was to assume its leadership. She accompanied Rudolf Steiner on his numerous lecture tours around the continent and, with her troupe, demonstrations were given of some of the pieces which were being practised. Most frequently, however, it was on the simple stage of the Schreinerei that the early work was performed.

Another important element introduced by Steiner in these early days came in his second major training seminar in August of 1915. At that time he initiated what he called 'Apollonian eurythmy' in contrast to what he later brought forward as 'Dionysian eurythmy.' In these two polar elements are represented the differing relationship of the human 'I' to the world. In the Apollonian, the natural laws underlying the outer structure and forms of nature is prominent. The hidden spirit manifesting through the laws of nature, of geometry, of grammar are revealed. The

A glimpse of the stage inside the first Goetheanum

Apollonian speaks 'to' me of the wisdom of the spirit, coming as if from without.

The Dionysian, on the other hand, represents the inner soul quality of the 'I.' In Dionysian eurythmy that which moves the soul is expressed. In this element it is 'my' relationship to the things of outer nature which is prominent, the wisdom of the world and of the spirit as expressed 'through' me. The exploration of the Dionysian element has become especially prominent in modern dance though often in a 'fallen' manner similar to the Greek Dionysus cults dating from an era when the Mysteries had already gone into decay. The mistake of taking these explorations too deeply into the physical body is that instead of exploring the fieriness and freedom of individual creativity, one instead sinks into expressing the passionate fires of the lower nature in the human being, a place in which one finds oneself not free at all but merely the pawn of one's baser instincts. Steiner wanted eurythmy to be balanced between both these poles of Apollo and Dionysus while remaining in the free space above the realm of compulsion.

By 1919, the work had progressed far enough to enable a staging of the first full-length performance. Given in a theatre in Zurich in February of that year, the performance consisted of primarily non-musical pieces (some had musical preludes) though in later performances a balance between musical and speech pieces was often sought. The early eurythmy programmes often followed a progression from more serious or solemn works in the beginning with lighter fare and humoresques to conclude the evening. At this time, pieces tended to be shorter in length but as the art form evolved longer, more ambitious pieces were able to be staged.

In 1919, performances were given throughout Switzerland and Germany, and later throughout Europe. Steiner began creating forms for languages other than German — in English, French and Russian — with indications as to how one expresses the unique qualities of the sounds in these languages. In time eurythmy schools arose in Paris, in Stuttgart, and in the Netherlands. In later years as interest

The Eurythmeum in Stuttgart (rebuilt in 1964).

in the art grew, schools sprang up in England, South Africa, Scandinavia, the United States, Japan and, most recently, in Russia.

The work deepened with the expansion of eurythmy into educational and therapeutic applications as well as with Steiner's continued teachings culminating in his two lecture courses in 1924 (published under the titles of *Eurythmy as Visible Speech* and *Eurythmy as Visible Song*). Further courses were scheduled but never occurred due to his death in March of 1925.

After his death, Marie von Sievers-Steiner continued to shepherd the young art and slowly to watch it grow. With most of the work centered in Central Europe, the coming to power of the National Socialists was very disruptive. Because of their connection to the frowned upon anthroposophical movement (whose spiritual impulse was in opposition to the occult impulse of the Nazis), eurythmists were to receive anonymous death threats and, in 1941, eurythmy was officially banned in Germany — the teachers in the Stuttgart eurythmy school were even ordered to work in nearby textile factories! The devastation wreaked by the war was to leave few resources for supporting the arts, and eurythmy was to quietly languish while the continent rebuilt.

In the 1960s the work began rapidly to expand. Grand stage companies were born in Dornach, Hamburg, Stuttgart, Munich and in the Netherlands, along with smaller innovative ensembles in other centres in Europe and North America. Groups of eurythmists were incorporated into several operas — their value in convincingly portraying spiritual or even netherworlds was recognized by directors after Steiner. Entire symphonic works were made visible through eurythmy in such works as the Goetheanum stage troupe performing Beethoven's *Leonore Overture* or the Stuttgart group's rendering of Schubert's *Unfinished Symphony* with the collaboration of the Romanian State Orchestra. Steiner was able to solve the difficult staging of Goethe's *Faust* through the use of the possibilities of eurythmy. After his death, other major dramatic and poetic works were to be accompanied or even entirely rendered through eurythmy from Dante's *Divine Comedy* to Strindberg's *Ghost Sonata* to some of the short plays of Thornton Wilder to the epic *Peer Gynt* — all were given a new

Dante's Divine Comedy *(Stuttgart Eurythmeum group)*

interpretation and even revolutionary impact in their trans-
figuration through tableau of movement.

As this narrative has brought us up to the present, it
might be helpful to switch from a historical to a descriptive
perspective of this stage art. Though it is well-nigh impossible to picture eurythmy through only a written description,
we will nevertheless attempt to characterize a performance
as well as to examine some of what lies behind it.

A stage performance

As the curtain opens, we are generally met by an empty
stage with plain backdrop curtains where its only ornament
is the illumination of the lighting. Eurythmy tends not to
rely on stage props or decorations but rather to evoke the
imaginations of place and context through costume, lighting,
and the weaving of movement. As the performers glide onto
the stage, usually facing the audience, the lighting may
change, ushering in an entirely different mood. We are
struck by the long silk dress and transparent silk veil which
is draped over the arms and shoulders, especially in the way
they assume the varying colour moods. In a moment we

Peer Gynt *performed by the Stuttgart Eurythmeum*

will look more closely at costume and lighting, but for now let us remain with this first impression.

We cannot help but notice how the performers do not so much walk or run but float across the stage. The earlier mentioned technique of 'threefold walking' enables a seemingly gravity-free passage through space (unless the piece specifically demands a weightiness), an effect which almost imperceptibly lifts us out of our own heaviness. We sense a breathing relaxedness, a lightness, and a freedom of movement, free either to ascend to the heights or to delve into the dark depths (without the distracting and somewhat crude necessity of leaping into the air or rolling around on the floor). This uplifted feeling also stems from the higher centre of gravity from which the eurythmist takes her movement. The student of Tai-Chi or the martial arts learns to sense the source of movement in the *tan t'ien,* a centre three inches below the navel, while many in ballet and modern dance have come to follow the injunction of Isadora Duncan to move from the solar plexus. In eurythmy, movement is carried through the collar bone, allowing the arms to sing from this plane and the rest of the body to follow. The focus of our attention tends to be the expressiveness of the arms and hands. With the legs clothed in a long gown and even the most subtle movement of the arms accentuated by the rippling of the veil, we are drawn into the language of these limbs moving winglike through the air. To an audience accustomed to the footwork of ballet or the 'legginess' of modern dance, this contrast can be disconcerting. The arm movements are harmonious (even in strength or great speed), rounded, full, engendering confidence and power without forsaking the potential for subtle expressiveness. Here we most readily experience the working with etheric movement, the movement quality of livingness. In this veritable flowing stream of continuous motion the moving veils seem to create cloudlike forms which immediately dissolve only to reveal others which again disappear. Fixed positions are rarely assumed as one would in ballet, rather an entire piece tends to be an unbroken line of movement from the performers' entry on the stage until their exit (even a pause is filled with charged motion). We note the lack of the technical virtuosity which a dance performance may highlight — the eurythmist may lend an intensity to a series of movements or accent with a dramatic gesture but the movement shies away from athleticism and the harmony of the group's united endeavor is stressed — an individual's technique should not dilute the common imagination which is created.

The choreography of the moving figures can be confusing at first as we attempt intellectually to grasp at its meaning. The nature of the 'revealed laws of nature' of which we earlier spoke are not intellectually but rather artistically rendered and more subtly than directly presented. In this constant weaving of metamorphosing movement, patterns only gradually emerge and more often to the eyes of the feelings than those of analytical thinking. However, as we begin to sense the dynamics of what is in essence one breathing organism rather than focusing on minutiae, we feel lifted out of everyday consciousness onto that plane of living movement. We move inwardly with the life of this organism opening to impulses and understandings that our mundane lives often leave little room for. The sensitive observer meditatively tastes Steiner's intent to 'take what lives in Spirit and ensoul it in eurythmy.'

It is clear that like opera, ballet, or even the symphony, such an appreciation may not be immediate but require cultivation on the part of the viewer before such an unlocking of the mysteries of the art form may occur. What eurythmy would grant the viewer is the gift of a spiritual imagination which does not remain fettered to the limitations of intellectual thinking but is experienced even in the body. Essential in firing these imaginations with mood and feeling as well as life are the glowing and vivid colours in which the whole is bathed and even immersed. We should at this point look more closely at that aspect which we have so far postponed, the role of costume and lighting.

Costumes and lighting

In the spirit of the *Gesamtkunstwerk*, the impulse shared by Wagner and other artists of the turn of the century to create a 'total work of art,' in eurythmy nothing is unessential — the dress worn on stage and the lighting are integral parts of the total experience. As we mentioned, the traditional garb for the eurythmist is a long, loose, flowing silk gown with another transparent silk veil draped over both arms (and pinned at the wrists). This is not, as some have thought, to somehow mimic Isadora Duncan's hearkening back to the dress of the ancient Greeks or to capitalize on the success of the veils used by Loie Fuller in her performances, especially her famous butterfly costume (in which she extended the span of her arms with sticks to which the veils were pinned). Though Steiner was aware of these innovations, he had deeper non-theatrical reasons guiding the design of the costumes.

The tightly fitting leotard of many dancers inevitably brings the attention of the audience to the wonderful athletic physique, to the beautiful and even sexy body. In our time, fashion, athletics and dance have all been part of a move toward a sort of cult of the physical body. The dance of the

Mystery temple, however, had quite a different emphasis and intent — it sought instead to lift attention (and thereby consciousness) out of this physical realm to the etheric level, that of the rejuvenating life forces. While tightly fitting garments that follow the lines of the body accentuate the individual and the physical, the loose flowing dress of the eurythmist (which could be said to follow the ever mobile aura of the etheric body as it clings loosely to the physical) de-emphasizes the shapes and curves of the performers and instead directs awareness to the flow of the group's sculpting of space. Because the lower limbs are covered, they can be forgotten and, instead, the more delicate, expressive, and controlled movements of the upper limbs can be focused upon. Even the physicality of the arms is dissolved by the transparent veil which, cloudlike, surrounds them.

Variations on the classic garb may include headpieces, loose flowing trousers and tops, abandoning the veil, or even elaborate pinnings of additional pieces to the traditional gown. Always, however, there remains allegiance to the principle of not fixing the imagination too firmly by making the costume too realistic (the focus should be soft, dreamlike, suggestive rather than definitive) or cling too much to the physical. For in this manner the creative imagining of the viewer remains active and a receptivity to the supraphysical made possible.

Like Goethe before him, Steiner felt that colour had definite spiritual and even moral qualities. Through the studied and careful (though by no means conservative) use of colour he sought to accentuate the desired creation of a moment when the veils between worlds is parted, unfolding activities of the subtler spheres into phenomenal existence. Even further, Steiner perceived concordances between the individual colours and planetary and zodiacal forces or influences — these were to serve as a kind of 'subtext' to the use of colour in eurythmy, held in the back of one's mind when choosing colours and sometimes used more directly with this as a focus.

The use of colour in eurythmy takes place on many

Murs, ville,
Et port,
Asile
De mort,
Mer grise
Où brise
La brise,
Tout dort.

Dans la plaine
Naît un bruit.
C'est l'haleine
De la nuit.
Elle brame
Comme une âme
Qu'une flamme
Toujours suit!

La voix plus haute
Semble un grelot. --
D'un nain qui saute
C'est le galop.
Il fuit, s'élance*,
Puis en cadence
Sur un pied danse
Au bout d'un flot.

La rumeur approche,
L'écho la redit.
C'est comme la cloche
D'un couvent maudit; --
Comme un bruit de foule,
Qui tonne et qui roule,
Et tantôt s'écroule,
Et tantôt grandit.

Dieu! la voix sépulcrale
Des Djinns!... Quel bruit ils font!
Fuyons sous la spirale
De l'escalier profond.
Déjà s'éteint ma lampe,
Et l'ombre de la rampe,
Qui le long du mur rampe,
Monte jusqu'au plafond.

C'est l'essaim des Djinns qui passe,
Et tourbillonne en sifflant!
Les ifs, que leur vol fracasse,
Craquent comme un pin brûlant.
Leur troupeau, lourd et rapide,
Volant dans l'espace vide,
Semble un nuage livide
Qui porte un éclair au flanc.

Ils sont tout près! -- Tenons fermée
Cette salle, où nous les narguons.
Quel bruit dehors! Hideuse armée
De vampires et de dragons!
La poutre du toit descellée
Ploie ainsi qu'une herbe mouillée*,
Et la vieille porte rouillée
Tremble, à déraciner ses gonds!

Choreography by Else Klink for the poem Les Djinns *by
Victor Hugo*

levels for the language of colour is that of the enlivened imagination. As such, the training of this imagination is an essential part of the curriculum. Outwardly, however, the use of colour is seen primarily in the costumes and the lighting. To begin with, silk is normally the cloth of choice for the costume not only because of the fluid flexibility of the fabric but because of its sheen, its unique ability to act as a true vehicle of colour while acting as well to give a kind of texture to the colour. Steiner once described silk as being composed of fibres into which the tiny silkworms have literally woven light.

The way in which colours are picked for a piece is not merely by chance. Steiner designed a series of wooden figures, each painted in three colours, in order to illustrate the qualities engendered in the eurythmical gestures for the sounds of the alphabet. Each figure portrayed three basic qualities — the flow of *Movement* of the sound (in the colour of the dress), its qualitative *Feeling* (expressed in the colouration of the veil), and its *Character* (which showed the intensity with which the movement is made in all or part of the body or the degree of tension one must exert). This same approach could be used to describe the qualities of an entire piece of music or verse. Of course, the eurythmist cannot constantly change costume to represent the change that each letter or even aspect of the piece would bring. Instead, one choice of costume and veil colour is attempts to capture the essence of the piece. The opportunity to bring forth variations in mood and feeling comes through the use of stage lighting.

Due to his early education in the Vienna Technical Institute, Steiner always maintained a lively interest in new technologies. Like Loie Fuller, he was fascinated with the new possibilities which electrification of stage lighting would bring toward metamorphosing the stage space from earthly to supersensible planes. The saturation of space with colour which these powerful lights were capable of was the only 'prop' he required in order to 'set the stage.' As such, Steiner insisted on state-of-the-art lighting systems on his stages, a tradition maintained in the rebuilt concrete

Goetheanum which replaced the destroyed wooden original, and in the home stages of most eurythmy troupes. In the standard forms which Steiner choreographed for speech and tone eurythmy, he considered the costume colours and the lighting as an integral part of the whole. When he annotated the text or score, he gave exact instructions as to what the lighting should be (for both footlights and the overhead lights), as well as where changes should occur.

Through movement somehow freed of gravity and yet still in relationship to the earth, bathed in ever-changing hues and moods, this new stage art aspires to explore that aspect of experience which is truly human. The mythological picture of the centaur recognizes the dilemma of the human condition as half beast and half human (or even half angel). Whereas modern dance has somehow sought more to delve into the former, it is to the latter, to the truly human part, that stage eurythmy focuses its emphasis. In the course of this exploration it quickly became obvious that if the working into the physical human being of spiritual impulses could be artistically solved, that it could also make an important contribution to some of the problems in education and in the art of healing. For in both of these areas the dilemma is one of trying to figure out how this angelic humanity is to be incarnated into the physical beast or body in such a way that the angel uplifts the beast and not that the beast pulls down the angel, and to do so in a balanced manner which honours both these polarities. In these next two chapters we will look at how eurythmy strives to accomplish this through education and movement therapy.

4. Eurythmy in Education

In 1913, Rudolf Steiner was approached by Emil Molt, owner of the Waldorf-Astoria factory in Stuttgart. Molt asked Steiner whether he might start a school for the children of the factory workers based on the principles of his spiritual teachings. Steiner took up the task with enthusiasm and from the prototype which was established in Stuttgart there later sprang the international movement of Waldorf or Rudolf Steiner schools.

The curriculum of the Waldorf schools contains the subjects taught as other schools with two notable exceptions. Steiner added two new subjects to his schools, form drawing and eurythmy. A pedagogical eurythmy was thus to develop alongside the nascent art form, built on the same fundamentals but modified to address the specific needs of the growing child. Steiner considered eurythmy an essential subject from the start of the Waldorf schools (while interestingly leaving out physical education until later) and not merely a less important adjunct. In striving to comprehend why its role was considered so central, it would be useful to examine it alongside the other new subject, form drawing, as well as to contrast it with the more traditional teaching of movement in schools: physical education and gymnastics.

Form drawing and eurythmy

Form drawing consists of the drawing of continuous rhythmical patterns, initially as continuous line patterns and later as closed forms. In the early years these patterns may be rounded like a line of gentle hills or wave shapes or more

Emil Molt

angular as in the Greek key pattern. These form drawings are of the sort seen to ornament pottery and the borders of garments since earliest historical times. Their significance was apparently not merely decorative but rather the deeply experienced representation of the pulsing of life forces, of the manifestation of higher laws.

In the Waldorf curriculum, one could very narrowly understand the purpose of form drawing as helping the child to gain physical control of its hand movements as a precursor to cursive writing, a kind of 'writing readiness' exercise. On another level, however, the cultivation of the grace and the delicate but disciplined control which must be developed in order to do form drawing beautifully carries deeper learnings for the child. Form drawing requires control but not one involving strength or toughness. Rather an attentiveness to inner process is needed, a listening to the rhythms that pulse and breathe cyclically within and then a carrying of this impulse into the drawing of the forms. The process involved in the exercise is inextricably entwined with the result. One could attempt to draw such forms exactly via

measuring and drafting devices or the plotting of points but
this is precisely what is not intended. The facility to do
these drawings freehand necessitates a fostering of an inner
sense of harmony and balance. The child normally has some
inherent capacity for harmony and wholeness but it needs
to be further encouraged and sheltered as it grows. Childhood traumas, hereditary physical impairments, the intrusive
barrage of electronic media, and generally too much
exposure to the adult world too soon all serve to unsettle
this healthy core of the child — form drawing draws upon
and empowers this aspect of the soul of the child. As in
handwriting analysis, the emotional or soul challenges of the
individual are evident in form drawing. Similarly, just as
handwriting therapy can work very powerfully on correcting
the blocks that arise, so does form drawing have a similar
therapeutic role. It requires tremendous effort on the part of

Examples of form drawing with straight and curved lines

an adult to change one's handwriting or to learn calligraphy because certain habits have rigidly fixed themselves in the way a person uses one's life energies. The habits of writing are enmeshed with emotional habits and yield only with difficulty. To restore flow, movement, a breathing continuity and harmony to the drawing can be an excruciating chore because at some level an inner confrontation with the 'anti-life' habits which have been assumed is necessary. In the child where habits and ways of doing things have not yet become so fixed or set, the practice of form drawing is an intervention which helps to counter these forms of rigidity before they become too entrenched.

Like form drawing, eurythmy also works with how the life forces manifest in the human body and endeavours to keep them lively, flexible, and energetic. Both eurythmy and form drawing could be thought of as similar to the stretching exercises of the athlete or dancer but their aim is to keep mobile not only the physical body but also the soul of the child. The curriculum of both subjects accompany the child developmentally through the years of schooling, attempting to guide the new forces which the child is constantly acquiring and staving off the tendencies to harden, to cramp, to withdraw or avoid — all defences developed in response to the stresses of life which hamper the individual in later life. This relationship between the emotional life and the body has been much discussed in medical and psychological literature in the past decades. In his classic study, *Character Analysis,* the psychiatrist Wilhelm Reich described the dysfunctional assumption of what he called 'body armour' in the child's attempts to cope with stress. This armour consists of habits of posture and holding of muscular tension in parts of the body. While the armouring initially performs a protective function, it later freezes in place, serving as a barrier to free movement and the unfolding of future capacities. While unable on its own to entirely avert this cramping of the psyche and even malformation of the body, eurythmy can serve as an important antidote in preserving the soul health of the child. Because eurythmy confronts the inflexibility of these blocks so directly (especially in the situation where a child has only joined the Waldorf school in a later class), it can be a most challenging subject to teach — the preadolescent years can be very difficult when the children are already facing enormous changes in themselves and their bodies. The eurythmy teacher must be able to embrace these with positivity, enthusiasm and humour.

As artistic disciplines, form drawing and, even more so, eurythmy have a special relationship to the spiritual, archetypal realm for the arts, once personified as the seven Muses, serve this role of bridging the physical and spiritual worlds. These eternal archetypes manifest both in the eurythmy forms — the pattern the child moves — and in the gestures of arms and legs that are enacted. In the forms we see patterns which have found their place in the sacred dances of all cultures — the spiral, the circle, the square, the five and seven-pointed stars, as well as the movement of the contracting and expanding circle. Within the speech and tone eurythmy gestures, another level of archetypes is performed as sounds of speech and tones of music are expressed in gestures that echo the larynx's sound forming and shaping of the air. These archetypes provide models for healthy development, templates for the acting of the spirit within the physical plane in the tradition of the actor or dancer serving as the inspired mouthpiece of the gods. In repetitively imitating and practising these movements, they are subtly incorporated into the child's makeup, providing a structuring, an organizing of the child's energies, which effects even the physical formation of the brain and organs. For many a modern child, this healthy structuring is no longer occurring in any other way — with the demise of so many rhythmical games like skipping, clapping games, and folk dancing, some of the traditional sources of this morality building impulse have disappeared, being replaced by what could only be called 'soul-negating' activities. The result is a generation of more and more overweight children who exercise too little and take in impulses of entirely a different sort from the hours they spend in front of the television and Nintendo, impulses of questionable morality and with an emphasis that is onesidedly cerebral. Eurythmy provides such patterning for the child which later aids in developing concentration, self-discipline, and a sense for beauty. Through eurythmy the child is guided to a healthy body and a healthy soul.

Eurythmy and physical education

In most schools except for the occasional folk dancing, physical education (sports, gymnastics, etc.) is the only form of movement offered. The importance of physical education in the curriculum was recognized by Rudolf Steiner but he saw its function as complementary to that of eurythmy. Usually the reasons given for having physical education in schools are such generalities as the children's need for exercise, providing some change from all the sitting in academic lessons, or that it somehow helps to build self-esteem through the mastery of the body. Without negating any of these, Steiner envisioned a grander purpose for physical education. In one of his education lectures Steiner explained:

> By means of gymnastics and sport human beings fit themselves into external space, adapt themselves to the world, experiment to see whether they fit in with the world in this way or that ... (it) is not a revelation of humanity, but rather a demand the world makes upon the human being that they should be fit for the world and be able to find their way into it.[9]

Physical education is thus a training that prepares the child to stand upon the physical earth, to connect to the physical space around. Eurythmy, on the other hand, solicits the inner human being, training the soul nature of the child. Eurythmy seeks to be a soul gymnastics in contrast to the physiological gymnastics of physical education. Whereas the movement in sports trains the child to put their will into the

Gymnastic exercises developed by Rudolf Steiner and Count Bothmer

physical realm, eurythmy teaches the placing of the soul into the world. This includes qualities like passion, enthusiasm, sensitivity, warmth, qualities which can without the proper encouragement become locked within the child and never freely expressed. Eurythmy distinguishes itself through the fact that every movement is 'ensouled,' that every movement is at the same time the expression of the soul, just as the sounds of speech are an expression of the soul. Whereas physical education orients the child in physical space, the 'ensoulment' of movement involves an orientation in the realm of the spirit. For most individuals, and especially for children, movement is something done only half consciously and connected to this is the fact that thinking is similarly done only in partial awakeness. Rudolf Steiner's conception was that education should strive to awaken the individual making their lives open to spiritual inspiration rather than stumbling through life only partially awake, and thus unconsciously prey to other impulses. Hence:

> ... we can also guide the child's outer movements
> so that they become purposeful movements,
> movements penetrated with meaning, so that the

child does not merely splash about in the spirit in its movements, but follows the spirit in its aims. So we develop the bodily movements into Eurythmy.[10]

Eurythmy also has a role in the moral education of the child. On the one hand, the training in moving artistically with a group requires not so much individual prowess or mastery as much as a sensitivity and a listening to the other. To move harmoniously with one or more partners is a concrete practice in developing cooperation and sympathy for the individual differences of others in a manner more refined than one can realize in most physical education. This is because eurythmy is preeminently the 'social art' — while constrained to the physical body, each person remains stuck in individuality, but when lifted through the movement into the shared etheric space, the laws of a social realm are revealed.

On a more profound level, the development of grace in movement requires a subtle inner listening in order to perceive the often subdued voice of spirit which guides such movement. Fostering this inner ear leads the child to an aesthetic sensibility, a feeling for beauty and goodness as guiding life principles. Steiner rather strongly criticized the excessive pursuit of sports:

Theoretical Darwinism is to assert that man comes from the animals. Sport is practical Darwinism; it proclaims an ethic which leads man back again to the animal.[11]

Eurythmy can correct this extreme view by reminding the child of its spiritual or angelic origin manifested in the graceful, harmonious human being in motion.

A rod exercise with children

The curriculum

The eurythmy curriculum seeks to accompany the child developmentally through its stages of growth, aiding the child's undertaking of the challenges of each stage. As such it joins the rest of the curriculum of the Waldorf school in moving towards this goal. The subjects studied are tailored to address the particular capacities which need to unfold in the gradual process of the spiritual being of the child taking charge of the physical body inherited from the parents. The eurythmy lesson follows the themes of the other lessons — exploring Greek rhyme and meter when the child studies Greek history, practising certain geometric forms as the child studies them in geometry, or exploring forms for the four elements as they are introduced in the beginnings of chemistry. At the same time, however, it makes its own unique contribution to the incarnation of the child, of taking the spirit *in carne,* into the very flesh of the human being.

Children practising for a school performance

Steiner outlined a specific curriculum for eurythmy from pre-school through the secondary school years which addresses both the need for physical and social skill attainment. In the early years the lesson is presented as a kind of a story with gesture and movement or in play, while after the fourth class the lesson becomes more disciplined as the basic principles of speech and tone in eurythmy are built up and practised. By the end of the secondary school years the child is able to be part of a full fledged production of artistic merit.

The value of eurythmy within the school curriculum increases as the problems within education continue to multiply. More and more children with emotional and learning difficulties, and the need to balance the lives of even average children struggling with the stresses of increasingly fast paced and unbalanced times, have solicited

Training to be a eurythmist

from eurythmy a hygienic role in addition to its educational one. On another level, however, eurythmy has been developed to serve as a specific medical therapy. We shall now turn to these applications of the art.

5. Eurythmy as a Healing Tool

Eurythmy as a stage art has made great strides since its simple beginnings earlier in the century. Similarly, the applications in the field of education have flourished, no doubt due to the increasing popularity of the many hundred of Waldorf or Rudolf Steiner Schools, including those for children with special needs.

By contrast, eurythmy therapy could be seen as the little sister of the others. It began later and has developed more slowly, though in recent years, with the postmodern realization that allopathic medicine and the traditional medical model may have marked limitations, there has been a renewed interest in all forms of 'body therapies,' including massage, yoga, dance therapy, various Chinese movement disciplines and eurythmy. In this chapter, we will look briefly at a history of its development and try to gain some understanding of what, for some, is the most mysterious manifestation of this art of 'ensouled movement.'

A new therapeutic approach

Educational eurythmy grew rapidly from its beginnings in the Waldorf Factory School in Stuttgart in 1913. The class teachers were quite impressed with the new subject which had been introduced to the curriculum through its helping the children to improved coordination and sense of rhythm as well as building up their general health and wellbeing. However, they were also surprised to see how through only one or two lessons a week the eurythmy had a positive influence on the temperamental difficulties and nervous conditions in the children.

Some eurythmists and physicians who had observed this approached Dr Steiner and asked whether some specific therapeutic interventions might not be designed from this foundation. His response came in April, 1921 with his presentation of a 'Curative Eurythmy Course.' The course was given as part of a larger training for physicians and medical students and was presented in collaboration with two eurythmists, Erna Wolfram and Elizabeth Baumann. Soon, the first experiments with an eurythmy therapy were meeting with success in the Waldorf School and in anthroposophic clinics and nursing homes in Stuttgart and Arlesheim (near Basel) as well as in the private practices of several physicians.

In 1922, he asked a medical doctor who had also studied eurythmy, Margarete Kirchner-Bockholt, to undertake leadership in the training of eurythmists in this new approach. She was able to work closely with Steiner over the next two years during which time he was able to give much practical advice regarding its potential for healing a variety of physical and psychiatric conditions. Steiner's illness and death in early 1925 brought this collaboration to an end but the work of developing eurythmy therapy continued. In looking at the broader picture of eurythmy's contribution as a therapeutic tool, there are actually two aspects which must be considered.

On one hand, there is the work done within the educational realm which has expanded to address both remedial and hygienic needs. On the other hand, there is the more specialized field which has evolved from the first 'Curative Eurythmy Course' in which eurythmy assumes the role of a medicament, prescribed by a physician after a diagnostic evaluation.

Remedial and hygienic eurythmy

As was earlier noted, the early Waldorf School teachers were impressed by the therapeutic nature of even the normal eurythmy lessons for the children in their classes. With the increasing numbers of children with special needs, school eurythmists have often been approached for help in designing a remedial programme for an individual child. The child's difficulties have often already been evident to the eurythmist — both learning and emotional problems usually are also manifest in the impaired movement of the child. Especially in cases of dyslexia and other language problems it has been found that addressing poor coordination in rhythm and timing goes a long way towards alleviating the learning problem. The English eurythmist, Jean Hunt, has done a great deal in this direction, combining traditional eurythmy with specialized exercises for spatial orientation, fine motor control, rhythm and sequencing, and attention to language. In working remedially, a eurythmist may utilize an extra lesson per week to help one or a few children to master what they had been unable to do in the normal lesson as well as adding some of these new exercises. These exercises can sometimes be utilized by a non-eurythmist though there is then always the danger of their being performed too mechanically or too 'physically' in a gymnastic sense. For the most possible benefit, these exercises, too, need to be ensouled and moved 'etherically.' For some children, such remedial interventions are insufficient and the more specific and in-depth eurythmy therapy may be required.

In many communities with a Waldorf school, there often is a demand for eurythmy classes for adults alongside other offerings of etheric movement like yoga or Tai-chi Chuan. All of these offer a certain amount of physical exercise and stretching for flexibility but, unlike sports activities, it is not physical strength but the rejuvenating aspects of the etheric or life body which are emphasized. For many, modern life brings an overload of stress and insufficient opportunity for non-mechanical enlivened movement. To move freely and spiritedly in the expression of Nature's forces within one can restore an element of balance missing in the lives of many. In the same way as it works with children, eurythmy also brings the benefit of fostering harmonious social relationships as one learns to move sensitively and in concord with other members of the class. Due to both of these qualities, the stimulation of life forces and the encouragement of social harmony, eurythmy has in recent years found specific applications in two arenas — within prisons and in the factory or workplace.

There have been numerous attempts to bring eurythmy as a social therapy to prisons. In a setting laden with the image of the human being as a caged beast, where the human spark is sometimes almost extinguished, eurythmy has shown itself capable of combating the tendency to cruelty and uncontrolled, instinctual behavior through providing an inner uplifting. Within the prison setting, it is not only physical but moral rejuvenation that is stressed, as a sensitivity for social awareness and harmony is cultivated.

For the worker, another form of dehumanization is often met in the technological workplace, whether in the drudgery of repetitive work with machinery, on the assembly line or at the computer screen, or in archaic management practices which reproduce an authoritarian master-slave relationship. The result can manifest in physical ailments or nervous disorders, or more subtly in the form of reduced worker productivity and job satisfaction. The recent move toward a Total Quality Management model in many workplaces has sought to address some of the latter issues through breaking down some of the power structures and promoting the need for better teamwork, for closer working relationships. As such, both of those qualities of individual and social enlivening which eurythmy promotes seem aptly suited to addressing the ills of the modern workplace.

In the Netherlands, 'The Institute for Eurythmy in Industry, Business, and Professional Life' was formed to deal with just these issues. Specially trained eurythmists have worked under their auspices in companies throughout

Europe and America, implementing courses for trainers within the company, with periodic sessions for the entire staff as well. Programmes are designed to address the needs of each setting (considering factors like the age group of the workforce, the kind of work being performed, etc.) which can later continue without the direction of the eurythmist. Participating companies have found improvement in staff concentration, tension release, and general improvements in health. However, a major benefit arises in the area of group harmony as the teams come to experience themselves as more of a community in performing this movement work together in a leaderless group.

Eurythmy therapy

The hygienic and remedial extensions of educational eurythmy can be sufficient in many instances to restore balance to an ailing organism, both individual and social. Their effect could be compared to the general health-giving function of eating a balanced and nutritious diet. However, when a specific and deeply seated constitutional problem must be

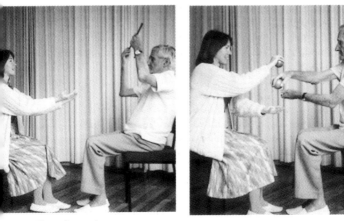

Eurythmy therapy

addressed, the more intensive eurythmy therapy may be needed. In this form of treatment, a physician examines the individual and, with the medical diagnosis, meets with the eurythmist and together they discuss which eurythmy exercises would be prescribed.

The principle underlying this form of treatment is that healing involves the restoration of imbalances in the individual. The etheric, life-giving forces with which eurythmy works, when directed to the particular region that is ailing, can combat the degenerative forces at work there. Such a therapeutic approach does not work like our common allopathic medicines that destroy bacteria or relieve pain through the deadening of sensation, but rather through seeking to stimulate the body's capacity to heal itself. Eurythmy therapy stirs the creative life forces into activity within the individual, forces which have become too sluggish or disordered to maintain health. Eurythmy therapy is a metamorphosis of stage eurythmy. Whereas they both work with the formative forces of the human being, in a performance these forces are directed outward while in the therapeutic capacity they are directed inward toward the ailing part of the individual. Like the early stage eurythmy, it is primarily the sounds of speech which are worked with (though there is a growing body of work involving therapeutic tone eurythmy). The formation of the sounds is modified, however, in order to serve a therapeutic rather than artistic end.

In Chapter 2 we saw the way that the speech sounds act as microcosmic reflections of the cosmic working of the life building and forming forces. When an artist presents a poem, a myriad of sounds is made visible in eurythmy gestures, one flowing into the next. However, when these forces are to be harnessed in the service of healing, the tendency is to choose one or a few sounds which emphasize that particular facet of these forces which the patient needs help in stimulating within. Through repetition of these sound gestures, the sick organism can be guided to renewed harmony.

A patient who comes in complaining of cramping from spending too long at the computer keyboard or in practising the violin might require the rolling, vibrating dynamic of the 'R' to rhythmically and gently restore movement to the overstrained muscles. For the child who is bedwetting, a firmness of control might be encouraged with the 'holding in' quality of the 'B'. The forces of the hard 'K', on the other hand, may be utilized for aiding the bowels to push in a case of constipation or, in a different application, to help push new teeth through the palate in an eight year old.

In contrast to the plastic, outer, form-building consonantal forces (forces which we commonly term 'the Laws of Nature'), the vowels tend to work more in an inner way on the emotional being of the patient, stimulating a kind of organic egoism or self-consciousness. This is accomplished through working on the breath and from there the other organic systems are effected. Exercises using the vowel sounds can help to overcome subtle difficulties of temperament or nervous problems. One sound (or series of sounds) may aid in promoting strength and purpose in a shy and withdrawn child while another may help to relax a high strung hyperactivity. On another level, treatments for epilepsy, psychotic disturbances, or migraine headaches may all include work with the vowels. In life, these inner and outer aspects are continuously interwoven. For this reason, the therapy for a specific problem almost always involves bringing several of these sound qualities to bear.

In addition to the sound gestures, exercises may involve the stepping or clapping to various rhythms or moving a specific geometric form. Accentuation of this movement might include repeating it at various speeds, first slow, then increasingly fast, and then slowing it down again. The form might also be strengthened by leading oneself through it holding a copper rod or ball. In one especially effective exercise for restoring harmony to the breathing and circulation, the patient moves along the lung-shaped 'harmonious eight' form, leading with a small copper ball. First the form is visualized standing, then moved only with the ball as the patient sways in accompaniment, and then moved with the entire body in larger and larger forms.

Through the few concrete examples that have been

Therapy for children with special needs

mentioned, one begins to get somewhat of a notion as to how this therapy works. To further illustrate it might be helpful to give a more complete example of an entire eurythmy therapy session.

A therapy session

A preadolescent child was referred to the eurythmist for help with a moderately severe case of scoliosis — curvature of the spine. The physician who had made the diagnosis was hoping that through eurythmy something could be done for the problem. In the early days of eurythmy therapy, students of various classes were grouped together and brought into the large hall or gymnasium, the groupings corresponding to similar developmental difficulties shared by the children. The therapist went around the hall, instructing a group at a time. The students then practised the exercises and returned to their classrooms. Only more severe medical difficulties (like the one which we will examine) were treated on an individual basis. Through the years it has come about that almost all children are now treated individually or in very small groups. A large Waldorf school in Europe employs three or four full-time eurythmy therapists, so important is their function viewed to be.

The therapist approaches the session by trying to warm the child with enthusiasm and humour. It is necessary for the child to relax a bit as well as for the child's will to heal to be engaged. In this case, after a hearty welcome, the therapist begins the twice weekly sessions with an idea from remedial work by having the child jumping rope. This not only serves to relax the child and act as a kind of 'ice-breaker,' but at the same time acts as a diagnostic tool to determine how the child is coming along. As the child jumps to the rhythm of a verse, the lack of sequencing ability becames evident as well as the contrast between upper and lower body coordination. The child's spatial awareness and posture are also found to be problematic.

After this warm up, they begin with an exercise to a simple verse with the three archetypal vowel sounds of 'I' (ee), 'A', and 'O.' With each line of the verse, the child jumps from one to the next position, in each position expressing one of the sounds in movement. Steiner had given this as a basic harmonizing exercise, one for 'snapping together' the physical and non-physical bodies of the individual and, in this case, as an aid to sensory integration or incarnation.

Next the child is led into an exercise with the consonant 'L.' This sound is one which is involved with molding the life forces in the body. Here it is to aid in stimulating flexibility in the spine and the muscles surrounding it. In an extreme scoliosis, the eurythmist might speak to the physician about the need for adjunctive measures like massage, body work, or occupational therapy, though the 'L' exercise often provides a sufficient 'loosening.'

The 'L' exercise begins with a gentle rocking back and forth on the balls of the feet, then slowly introducing the arms moving wavelike in the gesture of the 'L.' In eurythmy, movements are usually presented in imaginative pictures so that they are moved more dynamically and with the momentum of inner experiencing and not merely abstractly and mechanically imitated. The imagination of rocking in the waves gives the child a picture that can be easily entered and then gently massage the spine into movement.

After this warm-up, the work begins with the vowel sound 'I' (ee). The performing of this gesture outwardly involves the stretching of one arm diagonally upward while the other stretches downward as a balance. Depending on the direction of the curvature of the spine, the physician recommends which side needs more strengthening and therefore which arm need be the elevated one. This gently begins the straightening but not so much through the physical act of the stretching as by the gradual realignment of the etheric forces that have taken on the cramped habit of the scoliosis. In eurythmy, it is first these life forces which must be dynamically brought into movement and only afterwards can the physical body follow. Eurythmy works first on this subtle level thereby avoiding the 'intrusive' quality that can be associated with some forms of bodywork (Reichian, rolfing). The 'I' exercise may also be done with the legs, pointing the toes and stretching the leg outward — the child may do this while enacting a princess in her long robes pointing first one toe then the other as she displays her golden slippers to her court.

The child next does some simple exercises with the copper rod. Steiner gave a series of rod exercises which he termed 'Hygienic Exercises,' intended to stimulate a general feeling of balance and rejuvenation and, particularly, to serve as an aid to good posture — all important in this child's situation. Finally, the half hour lesson is ended with a verse while the child stands quietly listening. The child is often asked to rest (or even to lie down) for a short period afterwards in order for what has occurred to consolidate within the child. It should be noted that this description reflects one particular session — there tend to be differences from one lesson to the next and certain elements added or left out as the treatment progresses (in this particular treatment, work with the sound 'U' is later added).

The child continued the lessons over a period of a months in blocks, alternating seven weeks of practice with seven week breaks. Slowly some of the exercises were taught to the mother so that she could do them everyday with the child for a few minutes. In this particular case, the child was found (somewhat miraculously to one physician) to be free of the scoliosis when the therapy came to an end.

Therapeutic eurythmy could be thought of as encompassing a role between that of two existing disciplines, occupational therapy and dance therapy. On one side, occupational therapy works with medical science in helping to bring movement into the muscles where some impairment has set in, be it through disease, accident, or sclerosis, and where a re-education of bodily movement is called for. Eurythmy has often been found to work both more quickly and more deeply than occupational therapy in that it emphasizes not the 'outer' bringing of the muscles into movement but rather focuses on stimulating the inner forces which are the source of movement. It is after all the dampening or deadening of these forces which form the core of the problem (though in some situations, occupational therapy would still remain a treatment of choice).

In contrasting these two disciplines we could say that occupational therapy tends to address the physical more directly while in eurythmy the stimulation of the etheric, life forces is stressed. With dance therapy, we encounter the meeting of the patient's etheric, life forces with that of the emotional nature. Dance therapy has evolved in the latter half of this century through the work of modern dancers with hospitalized psychiatric patients. This work soon expanded to include a clientele with less severe diagnoses who nevertheless found emotional relief in using movement to express what was difficult with words alone in psychotherapy sessions. In this sense, dance therapy is somewhat of a misnomer; rather, mime therapy might be more accurate

A humoresque is often part of a stage performance

since mime is the art form which attempts to express content without the use of words. In recent years, the work of dance therapy with trauma victims has been impressive in helping to give a voice to stories bound up within individuals. In helping to set the story free, the clients felt an accompanying sense of freedom once more to pursue their lives. Eurythmy has similarly worked with success in this arena of soul illnesses, though the focus of this work has tended more toward the major mental illnesses in adults and with a wide variety of conditions with children. The connection between emotional illness and imbalances of the physical body which is only slowly being explored in traditional medicine has long been a focus. A number of psychiatric hospitals, cancer clinics, and private medical practices rely on eurythmy therapy for help in this regard.

One might contrast dance therapy with eurythmy by saying that eurythmy tends to work on an intellectually less conscious level. While in dance therapy one might enact a rising anger and breaking free of an invisible oppressing force perhaps culminating with the naming of that oppressive entity, in eurythmy the freeing would unfold less forcefully, more gradually, almost imperceptibly, more noticeable in retrospect. The eurythmist never intentionally seeks to elicit repressed feelings or memory (avoiding the dangers seen in the debates over 'false memories') but rather seeks to empower by fortifying the individual to face whatever they may encounter within or without. It is not uncommon for these things to emerge, however, because in our habits of movement we hold repressed energies in our physical tensions and postures (again I would direct you to the research of Wilhelm Reich, notably his highly regarded *Character Analysis*). One begins to unlock the strictures of habitual movement and free these energies through eurythmic movement even without focussing on them. In working with the archetypal regenerative forces within the eurythmy gestures, these archetypes are not merely 'pasted' or forced on the patient. Each person arrives at their own archetypal gesture, helping to build their own individual body image.

It is this healthy self-image (sometimes requiring some struggle to build) which is able to confront or transform negative memories or self-images should they emerge.

Therapeutic eurythmy slowly continues to grow as the acceptance of all these physical (and etheric) therapies becomes more widespread. There are training centers in England and Europe which physicians and qualified eurythmists may attend and increasing numbers are going for this advanced training. National professional organizations have formed in several countries to promote and represent the therapeutic art. Specialized research in new areas continues though the number of practitioners finding the time to do research is limited; some areas of promise have been in work with HIV/AIDS, cancer and with ailments of the eye. Though there are over a thousand eurythmy therapists currently in practice, this number is miniscule in terms of the need.

6. Toward the Future

The art of eurythmy sprang from a modern knowledge of the spiritual world at a time when human consciousness was sinking more deeply into materialism. In this context, eurythmy's task was one to which true art has always aspired: to bridge this divide, to draw inspiration from the spirit and to bring it into matter, into the physical world.

Since Rudolf Steiner's time, the gulf between a world-view encompassing spirit and one of materialism has if anything widened. Technology has mushroomed both in terms of creating instruments of mass destruction and in terms of its ability to bedazzle the physical senses and encourage consumerism. As has been suggested in the first chapter, even the art of dance, in its endeavour to address modern issues, has too often been seduced too deeply into the physical, into the body, into matter. On the other hand, an opening up of consciousness of the spiritual worlds has also been marked in the burgeoning New Age movement, in the interest in near-death experiences, in the spiritual revelations of channels and inspired clairvoyants, in the many books on angels and the realm of the soul. Attempting to bridge the gap between these two has not been so easy and, in attempting to do so, eurythmy finds that it needs to approach the soul denying materialism (which is the experience of today's individual) while at the same time not losing its soul, not being dragged into a physicality that extinguishes its inspiring light. Stage eurythmy, in particular, has had to struggle to remain true to its original inspiration. Rudolf Steiner was a clairvoyant who had developed his gift for seeing into the spiritual worlds through his own efforts. When he gave indications for the

From The Winds of Time *(English Eurythmy Theatre)*

performing of eurythmy, he took his impulse from this
living and immanent experience of spiritual reality. After
his death, this impulse was to be carried by those who had
studied personally with him and by his wife, Marie Steiner.
It was felt by many, however, that something began to be
lost, perhaps because Steiner died before he was able to
pass on more of the art (Steiner had planned to give five
more lecture courses on tone eurythmy alone), or because
those that followed were not always able to attain the
heights of his inspiration. The coming of the Second World
War also caused a major disruption in the work and it took
some time to regroup afterwards, perhaps sidetracking the
original impetus.

All these factors no doubt contribute to the challenge
with which eurythmy struggles of continuing to present
itself as an art form fully penetrated by the spirit. In some
situations, Steiner's indications are not adequately understood and interpreted dogmatically resulting in stage
presentations which lack vitality. In other instances, attempts to meet the reality of late twentieth century experience through the art fall flat — some performances seem
trapped in the mentality of an art form of the 1920s and

From The Winds of Time

thirties. Another danger entails the following of the stream of dance too deeply into physicality, an ever present temptation especially for the eurythmist who was first trained in modern dance. Fortunately, through such gifted artists as Else Klink, Lea van der Pals, Carina Schmidt, Werner Barford, and Elena Zuccoli, to name but a few, the Muse has continued to guide the stage work in new and creative directions.

The task of joining the spirit and modern existence can seem a Herculean endeavour, especially because of how materialistic society has become. Steiner had foreseen that the humanity of the late twentieth century and beyond would be less and less influenced and penetrated by the spirit. In sinking deeper into physicality, the individual becomes physically and emotionally sicker and even deformed, increasingly cut off from the nonphysical energies which stimulate, build, enliven, rejuvenate, and inspire. Some examples of this deterioration are seen in the increase in obesity (especially amongst children), the epidemic of learning disabilities, the decrease in social responsibility, and the subtle but no less disturbing deterioration of language and speech (a drying up of language so that it no

Else Klink

longer allows communication on a deeper or poetic level but only for the conveying of practicalities).

This state of affairs had had its impact even in the training of eurythmists. Where the training was at one time less formal and entailed a couple of years, it later became standard to have a four year training, now more frequently being extended to five years. Though the student of today is more 'in her body' — more athletic, more fit (which older eurythmists have commented has made the art faster, more physically intense) — for many the sensing of the spiritual impulse is slower to come, to penetrate. More and more students require eurythmy therapy because the hardening materiality of modern life has damaged their ability to serve as instruments sensitive to the subtle nuances of the life energies — though the modern physical body is more able, more articulated, the soul element has become less so.

Another challenge of modern life, of course, is financial support. Even the most popular contemporary dance companies seem constantly on the verge of bankruptcy. In a

form of movement lacking sexual appeal, the cult of star performers, or presence on television, it is even more difficult to garner the needed support. As a result, most performers are forced to spend too many hours earning a living otherwise, leading to a dearth of full-time performing artists or to dilettantism.

In the field of education, eurythmy also struggles with the vicissitudes of modern life. The bringing of a living art form to today's increasingly jaded child is no mean undertaking, and for a variety of reasons in many Waldorf schools the teaching of eurythmy is considered among the most difficult of subjects. The teaching material that was appropriate in the past just does not seem to have the same impact any longer (especially with the older child). The teacher must wrestle with finding ways to meet the post-electronic age — woes of impoverished language sensitivity, impaired rhythmical ability, and shortened attention span that typify the children of the last generations; woes

which fortunately eurythmy is quite adept at countering. With the adolescent there is the additional problem of making them experience an archetypally moral and social art form as somehow relevant and meaningful. Whereas idealism has traditionally been a hallmark of this stage of life, in our times this has all become somewhat twisted by the values of consumerism, by children having been forced to grow up too soon, and by the much touted breakdown of the family and its values.

Finally, in the field of eurythmy therapy (in addition to some of the above mentioned challenges which pertain to it as well) there is the pressing need for more research. As all forms of alternative medicine and healing come under attack by traditional medicine, there is more and more of a demand for proof of results beyond anecdotal evidence. For many artistic therapists, however, their work and research methodology are reluctant bedfellows. Nevertheless, the need to overcome this aversion is necessary if eurythmy therapy is to gain acceptance outside the limited anthroposophical circles. Perhaps, some 'consciousness raising' in regards to questions of research needs to be incorporated into the training of eurythmy therapists (just as it is in some of the other 'soft sciences' of psychotherapy and social work despite similar reluctance in that arena) as well as the encouraging of more research by physicians who utilize this adjunctive therapy

Eurythmy was founded over eighty years ago and yet it still views itself as a young art. As such, eurythmists are well aware of the shortcomings and imperfections of their practice today, for the ideal toward which they aspire is an exceedingly ambitious one — to bring the dance of the angels and archangels down to the earth while struggling with the limitations of a physical body. Rudolf Steiner felt that in this century only the very beginnings of this new art form would be possible, but that these fledgling steps were vital in order to begin to address some of the most distressing issues of our times. The bringing of the spirit down to earth and into the physical body, thereby transforming it, is the miracle which every eurythmist encounters in her training in the art, as well as every time she steps onto the stage, into the classroom, or into the patient's room. As we have detailed, the obstacles to this inviting in of the spirit seem if anything, to be growing. However, eurythmy has an important ally for in Steiner's words:

> the physical organism of the eurythmist becomes through the eurythmic movements a receptive organ for the spiritual world, for the movements want to come down from there. [He continues] ... If the development of humanity is to progress, we must undertake this consciously, the bringing down of the supersensible into the sense world. We have consciously to bring the human body, this body of senses into visible movement in a manner that up to the present occurred invisibly, unconsciously. Then we shall be consciously continuing along the path of the gods ...[12]

Indeed, if this impulse can be fulfilled, the ideal of the ancient dancers of the Mystery temple will again bear fruit, signalling a renewal for the arts and for all humankind.

From Come, You Spirits *(English Eurythmy Theatre)*

References

1. Spoken in conversation with the Russian painter, Margarita Woloshin in 1908. Eva Frobose, *Zur Entstehung und Entwicklung der Eurythmie,* Rudolf Steiner Verlag, Dornach, Switzerland 1982, p.10.
2. Joseph H. Mazo, *Prime Movers,* Princeton, New Jersey, 1977, p.68.
3. Rudolf Steiner, *An Introduction to Eurythmy,* Anthroposophic Press, New York 1984, Talk I.
4. *An Introduction to Eurythmy,* p.91.
5. *The Gospel of St John* (1:1-4)
6. *An Introduction to Eurythmy,* p.78.
7. Rudolf Steiner, *Eurythmy as Visible Speech,* Rudolf Steiner Press, London 1984, Lecture 15, p.226.
8. Wolfganng Veit, 'Eurythmy and its Beginnings', *Journal of Anthroposophy,* Spring/Summer 1987, p.18.
9. Rudolf Steiner, *The Kingdom of Childhood,* Anthroposophic Press, New York 1995, Lecture 6, p.108.
10. Rudolf Steiner, *The Foundations of Human Experience,* Anthroposophic Press, New York 1996, Lecture 13, p.201.
11. *The Foundations of Human Experience,* p.201.
12. Rudolf Steiner, *Balance in Teaching,* Mercury Press, New York 1990, p.40.

Photographic acknowledgments

English Eurythmy Theatre 94, 95, 101; Klaus Fröhlich 90, 97, 98; Hulton Getty 14, 17, 18, 21, 22 25, 27; Verlag am Goetheanum 10, 33, 34, 35, 36, 40, 54, 55, 69, 73; Thomas Poplawski 44; Aliki Sapountzi 75, 76, 77; Dietmar Strauß 8; Verlag Urachhaus 30, 51, 57, 58, 59, 60, 64, 96.

Further Reading

Rudolf Steiner's books or lectures:
An Introduction to Eurythmy, Anthroposophic Press, New York 1984.
Eurythmy as Visible Speech, Rudolf Steiner Press, London 1984.
Eurythmy as Visible Music, Rudolf Steiner Press, London 1977.
Curative Eurythmy, Rudolf Steiner Press, London 1983.

Books by other authors:
Dubach-Donath, Annemarie, *Basic Principles of Eurythmy,* Mercury Press, New York 1990.

Dubach-Donath, Annemarie, *A Eurythmist's Recollections of Rudolf Steiner,* Anthroposophic Press, New York 1950.

Kirchner-Bockholt, Margarete, *Fundamental Principles of Curative Eurythmy,* Temple Lodge Publishing, London 1992.

Poudeyron, Elizabeth, ed. *Eurythmy: Essays and Anecdotes,* Schaumburg Publications, Roselle, Illinois 1980.

Raffe, Harwood, and Lundgren, *Eurythmy and the Impulse of Dance,* Rudolf Steiner Press, London 1974.

Siegloch, Magdalene, *How the New Art of Eurythmy Began: Lory Maier-Smits, The First Eurythmist,* Temple Lodge Publishing, London 1997.

Eurythmy Training centres

United Kingdom
Eurythmy School
Peredur Centre for the Arts
Dunnings Road
East Grinstead,
W Sussex RH19 4NF

Ringwood-Botton
Eurythmy School
The Sheiling Community
Ashley,
Ringwood, Hants. BH24 2EB

West Midlands Eurythmy Ass.
63 Hall Street
Stourbridge,
W Midlands DY8 2DE

United States
The School of Eurythmy
285 Hungry Hollow Road
Spring Valley, NY 10977

Boulder Eurythmy Program
3655 Sunshine Canyon
Boulder, CO 80302

South Africa
Cape Town School of Eurythmy
37 Columbus Road
Claremont 7700

Germany
Schule für Eurythmische
Art und Kunst
Argentinische Allee 23
14163 Berlin

Marie Steiner-Akademie
Mittleweg 12
20148 Hamburg

Schule für Eurythmische Kunst
Brehmstrasse 10
30173 Hannover

Alanus Hochschule für Kunst
Johannishof
53347 Alfter

Institute fur Eurythmie
Annener Berg 15
58454 Witten-Annen
Germany

Eurythmeum Stuttgart
Zur Uhlandshöhe 8
70188 Stuttgart

Akademie für Eurythmische
Kunst München
Hauptstrasse 42
82284 Grafrath

Switzerland
Eurythmeum Elena Zuccoli
Hügelweg 83
4143 Dornach

Eurythmeum Dornach
Postfach 24
4143 Dornach

Heileurythmie Ausbildung
Postfach 134
4143 Dornach

Rest of Europe
Academie voor Eurythmie
Riouwstraat 1
2585 GP Den Haag
Netherlands

Eurythmieschule Järna
Rudolf Steiner Seminariet
Box 1654
15 300 Järna
Sweden

Centre pour Eurythmie
1 rue François Laubeuf
78400 Chatou
France

Bildungstätte für Eurythmie
Tilgnerstrasse 3
1040 Wien
Austria

Eurythmy Studio Mosow
Russia

Index

Figures in italics refer to illustrations

Rudolf Steiner: his Life and Work

An illustrated biography

Gilbert Childs

This is a concise illustrated introduction to Steiner's life and work, describing how many of his ideas have been put into practice and are still giving inspiration and guidance to many people.

Rudolf Steiner's Ideas in Practice

Each of the books in this series is an illustrated introduction to Steiner's ideas on a particular topic, showing how they are being applied in practice today.

Biodynamic Agriculture
Willy Schilthuis
Based on Rudolf Steiner's ideas on agriculture, biodynamics is now widely recognized as a successful branch of organic farming.

Living Architecture
Kenneth Bayes
Steiner was an early exponent of what has come to be called organic design in architecture.

Children with Special Needs
Michael Luxford
Steiner's ideas on the education of children with special needs have led to the creation of special schools, homes and communities throughout the world.

Renewing Christianity
James H Hindes
For Steiner, Christ's incarnation and death on Golgotha were central events in history. The author also describes The Christian Community, a movement for Christian renewal.

Waldorf Education
Christopher Clouder & Martyn Rawson
A basic introduction to the Steiner/Waldorf School and its philosophy. There are over 700 Steiner Waldorf schools in forty countries, making this the largest independent educational movement in the world.